BELFAST PUBLIC LIBRARIES

738 · 38 [1]

L E E

674073

D1140711

PORTRAITS
IN POTTERY

H. H. Costain

QUEEN VICTORIA

1837-1901

Brown saltglazed stoneware, 12 inches high, modeled and signed
by John Broad, produced by Doulton & Co., Lambeth, 1897.

PORTRAITS IN POTTERY

WITH SOME ACCOUNT OF PLEASANT
OCCASIONS INCIDENT TO THEIR QUEST

BY ALBERT LEE

THE STRATFORD COMPANY, BOSTON, MASS.

COPYRIGHT —— 1931 —— BY
THE STRATFORD COMPANY
Publishers
PRINTED IN THE UNITED STATES OF AMERICA

PRINTED BY
THE ALPINE PRESS, INC., BOSTON, MASS.

TABLE OF CONTENTS

TABLE OF CONTENTS

TABLE OF CONTENTS

LIST OF ILLUSTRATIONS

Where not otherwise indicated in the captions, the photographs are of objects in the author's collection. In the case of Kings, Queens and Emperors, the dates given after their names are the periods of their reigns. In the case of all others, the dates are of birth and death.

LIST OF ILLUSTRATIONS

LIST OF ILLUSTRATIONS

LIST OF ILLUSTRATIONS

PORTRAITS
IN POTTERY

PORTRAITS IN POTTERY

CHAPTER I

HEN I was a small boy, traveling about Europe with my parents, I remember well that my father never failed to enter and rummage about in any old curiosity shop that lay along our path. Indeed, if we spent several days in a town, he would make it a point to seek out the old curiosity shops, in whatever byways they might happen to lurk.

Then, as now, however, they seldom lurked; they seemed almost always to be established in strategic locations, not too far from where the eye of the traveler might, without undue effort, catch the glint of brass and glass through their grimy windows.

If I may judge correctly from my own feelings, I am inclined to believe that small boys are never enthusiastic about foreign travel. They derive no thrill out of Baedeker or Bradshaw. To them a church is a church for a' that, and a cathedral only more so. Miles of painted canvases by old masters or others spell only weary walking to the immature. Their thoughts are of the ball-field at home, and of their more fortunate playmates whose parents know better than to find pleasure in sleeping in a different hotel every other night. Museums and monuments

1

bored me painfully in those days; yet the recollections of my early travels, maturing like wine, afford me today a pleasure upon which I could set no price.

I remember that I accepted sight-seeing, which I had been told should be considered as a part of my education, as the burdensome part of traveling. Being educational, sight-seeing became a duty which had to be performed,—and was performed, with laggard foot and patient resignation. The days, or hours, which were not devoted to sight-seeing, were always more enjoyable or, to be more accurate perhaps, less distasteful. Into this pleasanter category, my memory places the visits to the old curiosity shops. Here, at least, a boy had some opportunity to exercise his sense of selection, his spirit of adventure, his innate curiosity.

True, his indulgence of these tastes was constantly censored by such parental exhortations as "Keep your hands off!" "Don't touch that!" "Put those glasses down!" "Don't play with that gun!" and other similar prohibitions in endless variety. Nevertheless, there was a mystery and a fascination about these dark recesses, those cultured caverns, that contributed a welcome variety to the dull business of doing Europe.

Strangely enough, my many visits to old curiosity shops never inspired me with acquisitive desires along any definite or particular line. At least, not at that time. My collector's bump remained dormant. It was perhaps developing; but it did not become active until many years later,—if we may except stamp collecting, which is a mild mania that sooner or later afflicts all boys, whether or not their fathers initiate them into the mysteries of continental junk shops.

This juvenile experience, however, undoubtedly had its effect; and, even though I did not appreciate it, I was unconsciously cultivating a taste for the sport of hunting the antiquary in his lair, which for so many years in later life has been a source of joy and delight.

There were no Antique Shops in those days. There were Old Curiosity Shops. The word "antique" had not yet become debased, depraved and debauched; robbed of its honor in the vocabulary of precise definition; degraded by association with vulgarity and fraud.

It was still an adjective. One spoke of antique furniture, antique glass, antique china. The word had not yet fallen into common use as a noun. It still retained the dignity of its classic derivation. Now, alas, it has fallen so low, through constant misuse, that even its significance has become weakened, for I frequently hear the vulgar speaking of "old antiques."

It is perhaps with words as with maidens. Once they go astray, none may foresee whither they may wander. From a pure adjective, the word "antique" has, by common usage, become a noun. It has wandered even further; it has become a verb. One speaks

3

now of "antiquing,"—meaning to hunt or search for antiques.

We might even carry a little further the simile of the maiden who goes astray. After the word "antique" had fallen to so low an estate as to become a verb, it produced, as sometimes occurs with erring maidens, a fatherless offspring,—a noun: "antiquer," —one who antiques, one who goes antiquing, or who searches for antiques.

So far as I know, this noun, and its definition, have not yet found recognition in the dictionary. Yet, no doubt, by the time the dictionaries of today are being collected by the antiquers of tomorrow, the latter will find themselves duly defined in the lexicons of their times.

Whether or not the word antiquer is as yet accepted by the Academy, there can be no denying the fact that antiquing has become the sport, the pastime, indeed in some cases almost the occupation of what seems to be a very large proportion of the population. In days not so very remote, a collector of anything was looked upon more or less as a sort of harmless lunatic. To take an interest in the gathering of old prints, or pewter, or glass, or china, was an obvious indication of approaching senility. The collector's friends considerately overlooked this regrettable display of a weakening intellect, but his mere acquaintances frequently chaffed him openly about the litter and junk with which he was encumbering his house.

4

AN OLD CURIOSITY SHOP IN VENICE

Not so now. One could almost believe that a new gospel had been spread in the land. One might suspect that some subtle prophet of an impersonal Shintoism had converted the multitude to a strange form of ancestor worship. For suddenly all those things that were our ancestors' have acquired extraordinary value; in most cases regardless of any quality or merit. I use the word "ancestors" in its most abstract sense; to indicate a period, rather than any individual or personality, for I know of no one who collects the possessions of his own ancestors, and I come almost daily into contact with those who seem to be gathering with avidity the furniture, glassware, and other relics of other people's ancestors. Indeed, the personality of the original possessors of these things which are now collected seems to be of no interest whatever to the ultimate possessor, except in such cases as the hundreds of teacups out of which George Washington drank, and the innumerable chairs in which Lafayette sat. Lafayette must have spent most of his time during his visits to New England seated in Windsor chairs, and Washington was apparently voracious for tea.

But it is perhaps only natural that there should be but little interest displayed in the individuality or personality of those who made, possessed and cherished the things which are now being collected. How can the majority of present-day collectors of early-Americana hold any real personal interest in early

5

Americans? There are not enough of these people who had American ancestors.

The new cult is one which might therefore be called broad. It accepts any or all ancestors,—provided they left any goods or chattels. The pulpits from which the faith is spread are the auction blocks of our city salesrooms; the shrines sought out by the devoteees are the thousands of antique shops that line our motor highways.

And, just as the fertile mesa is spoiled as a pasture for cattle when the sheep come there to graze, so the conditions, which, a generation ago, afforded opportunity and delight to the true collector, have been almost entirely changed by the rabble of unlearned and indiscriminate buyers of anything to which they can apply the much abused term "antique." The vast amount of rubbish which, in the past ten years, has been bought and sold under that designation, is sufficient to sicken the heart of anyone who has the slightest respect for the products of those craftsmen who worked with earnestness and sincerity in the days when Grand Rapids was still a prairie and quantity production an unknown crime.

It is perhaps idle, however, to deplore change, for, after all, change usually means progress; and while it may be true that today there are a hundred antique shops where twenty years ago there was but one old curiosity shop, it is probably just as true that the wise collector of the present has a hundred opportunities to secure a prize where his father had but one such chance. There are still many good things left. All the treasures have not yet been discovered. The stream still holds many a fat fish. The sport of antiquing is as good today as it ever was,—it is perhaps even better, for the constant stirring of the waters is daily bringing more fish to the surface. The trout will fall a prey to the skilful and experienced angler. The rabble will hook the minnows and the bullheads, as it always has in the past.

CHAPTER II

VERY collector, no doubt, finds it of interest to look back into his earliest experience and endeavor to determine when and how and why he first began to collect,—to recall what was the great inspiration, or the trifling incident, or perhaps the mere accident which sparked the flame that now lights his way from one glorious adventure to another.

In many cases the urge to gather a certain type of thing is aroused by the acquisition, either through inheritance or as a casual gift, or even by chance, of some object which so appeals to one's taste that a fervent desire is immediately engendered to acquire others of its kind. In some cases a partially formed collection comes into one's possession and creates the enthusiasm for its continuation and enlargement. In very many cases, probably in the majority of cases, the inspiration to collect comes from having seen, admired, and perhaps even coveted the accumulated treasures of another.

Not long ago, in examining my own china cabinets to determine which was the first piece that I ever acquired, I found, considerably to my surprise, that this was a very ordinary specimen of Swiss peasant pottery in the shape of a dog. I bought it at the age of fourteen at a street fair in Thun, paying for it ten centimes, or two cents. What it was about this dog that fascinated me, I do not know. He is not, from any viewpoint, a good dog. He is a quadruped, but a dog only by courtesy of the imagination. He is made of a coarse red clay, enlivened with an impressionistic slip decoration of blue and yellow, and covered with a really brilliant glaze.

But what is more strange than the mere acquisition of the piece, which after all has a comic appeal, is the fact that the animal has survived these many years, and still gazes blankly and stolidly into space, without a nick or a crack in his anatomy, and has never been lost, mislaid, or broken in all the vicissitudes of his adventurous career. He must be a very faithful dog; and as such deserves and holds my loyal respect and consideration.

When I qualify his career as adventurous, I do not exaggerate; for that dog, since I acquired him, fresh from some little pottery in the Canton of Bern, has traveled many miles by sea and by land; and how it is that he never got lost is far beyond my comprehension.

The answer probably is that he has spent much of his existence in trunks or packing cases, reposing in the darkness of basements or storage warehouses. Even this suggestion is not wholly satisfactory, as I remember, through the years, seeing him many times, in various widely separated places where I have lived; and so I know that he has frequently come up for air, and must indeed have braved many of

the perils that fall across the path of china dogs,—
particularly homely, unattractive china dogs, which
come under the feminine classification of trash.

After traveling all over Switzerland with me from
Thun, the dog must have remained with me while
I was at different schools in France and in Germany
during the two following years. He must have voy-
aged across the Atlantic with me when I returned
to America. He certainly followed me to Exeter
Academy where I spent three scholastic years. I remember seeing the dog at Exeter. I remember having
him at New Haven too. He must have dwelt four
years in the academic shades of the Yale campus.
But after that he no doubt slept for a long time in
darkness. He must have gone into a trunk with
photographs of football teams, old dance cards,
books and the usual jetsam of college memorabilia,
—while I set forth unimpeded to conquer the wolf,
from the vantage point of a hall bedroom in New
York.

I cannot definitely remember when I next saw
him, but he must have bobbed up serenely sooner
or later, always welcomed and always carefully as-
signed to some secluded nook or high shelf where he
would escape being classified as trash. At any rate I
cannot now recall when I did not occasionally see
him around somewhere, and today I know just
where he is, because he has now been duly classified,
labeled and catalogued. Strange to say, he is the
only one of his kind in my collection. I have many

KING CHARLES II AND
QUEEN CATHARINE

Earthenware dish, decorated in blue with portraits
of Charles II (1660-1685) and his consort,
Catharine of Braganza. Diameter, 18 inches.
Lambeth, 1662.

KING CHARLES II

Enameled earthenware jug, or sack bottle, inscribed
"CHARLS' THE 2d" and decorated with a half-
figure of King Charles II (1600-1685) in armour.
Lambeth, 1670.

Victoria and Albert Museum

varieties of dogs, mostly Staffordshire spaniels, poodles, coach dogs and whippets. But the Thun dog is in a class apart. He is a mongrel. He is of very common clay; he has no modeling to speak of. My taste in ceramics has improved since I first spent two cents on him. But he has character and individuality nevertheless, and now stands on a narrow shelf, all by himself, in a little cabinet that once was a large New England clock case; and on the shelf above him are some fantastically colored clay animals from Mexico, also bought at a street fair,—at the Easter fair in the Alameda in Mexico City. On the shelf below him are some little clay animals, from France —common peasant pottery,—virile and rough and unpretentious.

I conclude that my taste for acquiring pottery must therefore have first expressed itself on that occasion of the fair in Thun, when I was lured by this majolica dog. This taste remained dormant for several years, because my next ceramic acquisition was a little brown toby-jug, bought at Mory's Chophouse, in New Haven, in my senior year at college. I even sometimes doubt if it was any genuine fondness for pottery that prompted my purchase of this toby-jug. It may rather have been that the toby was associated in my mind with the recollection of many pleasant and convivial evenings around the big table at Mory's, and that I wanted the little brown jug as a sort of monument to those academic occasions that were about to fade into the past.

Whatever the motive, I bought the toby from Eddie Oakley, the proprietor, and paid him thirty-five cents for it. I could have taken one home with me in my overcoat pocket any evening, as a souvenir; but I never did. I don't think this was because I was any more scrupulous than many of my college mates, whose rooms were cluttered with "souvenirs." I think it was because I really wanted the toby, and therefore wished to possess a good specimen, without nicks and notches and cracks such as the majority of the little jugs were disfigured with, through hard and careless usage. So I got Eddie Oakley to pick out for me a good one from his stock, and I paid him for it, to the derision of certain ribald companions. Eddie asserted that he imported his own tobies from England, which was no doubt true, as he had come from England himself, and still imported his own ale and the most delicious of Cheshire and Cheddar cheeses.

Mory's fell into decadence in the late Nineties. Eddie Oakley sold out, and the famous old chop-house was finally closed. I have often wondered what became of all the tobies and pewter mugs and the willow-pattern plates. Perhaps some of them found their way into antique shops, battered and cracked as they were, and are now bringing prices far in excess of thirty-five cents.

It is with some satisfaction that I recall the fact that, when I acquired the toby from Eddie Oakley, I was particular to insist upon having an undamaged specimen. It was intuitive to want a perfect piece. This was not, at that time, an educated taste, as with the exception of the majolica dog, I had never bought any pottery before, and had never felt any particular interest in those ceramic things which now afford me so great a pleasure.

In later years, when I began to collect china and to study it, to learn more about its qualities and its beauties, the policy of acquiring only perfect pieces has characterized all my dealings. I have made it a rule never to buy a piece that was nicked, cracked or repaired. I cannot assert that I never have bought a faulty specimen, but on the other hand I have resisted the impulse to buy dozens of damaged pieces, that I really wanted at the moment. The few maimed objects that I number in my collection were either bought in haste, without giving that meticulously careful examination which a collector should give to every piece he buys; or they have become broken in the vicissitudes of packing and transportation. Fortunately, these are but very, very few, and such broken ones as I have retained have been most carefully restored as nearly as possible to their original condition, the result being that my jugs and statuettes are a clean looking lot with none of those ugly and defacing defects which so often detract from the charm of a china cabinet.

After years of experience in forcing myself to "pass up" damaged pieces, I am convinced that this is the soundest policy to be pursued by the modest

13

collector. I cannot now remember any damaged piece that I regret not having bought. Furthermore, I have parted with several imperfect specimens purchased in haste. I have literally compelled myself to get rid of them in order to maintain the standard imposed upon myself. I have no regrets over their loss, for it was not a loss; it was a gain, when one's collection is considered as a whole.

I remember well hestitating long and painfully over a Lord Rodney jug, which was offered to me by a dealer in London, and which I coveted deeply. I turned it over and over again in my hands, but it was seriously cracked and bore a couple of ugly nicks on the rim. True, set upon a high shelf, these defects would have been apparent to no one,—but I should always have known that the jug was cracked and nicked, and I could never have rejoiced in its possession. I never could have handled it with affection, and joy. I never could have let a friend examine it without apologizing for its imperfections.

"No, thank you," I finally said to the expectant dealer, "I can't take it. It's damaged."

"But I am offering it to you at a damaged price," he replied persuasively. "If it was a perfect piece, it would be cheap at five pounds. You may have it for thirty bob."

I hesitated; but finally pushed Satan behind me.

"I make it a rule never to buy a damaged piece," I said, bravely; "not at any price. If you offered it to me for a shilling, I should still decline to be tempted."

"But you can't find a jug like this that is not damaged a little. They're all damaged," argued the dealer. "You must expect a few defects here and there. This is over a hundred years old; it has been used and handled. It is only natural that it should bear a few evidences of age and use. Why, these cracks really add to its value; they prove it is an antique and a right one."

But I was firm, and finally convinced the dealer that I could not be persuaded. I bought several things from him on other occasions, and got to know him and his shop quite well. I used to look in on him occasionally with the query:

"Anything in my line today?"

And more often than not he would smilingly reply:

"Yes, I've got something in your line, I expect, but you won't buy it. It is a figure of Shakespeare, but he lacks three fingers of the left hand."

Indeed the perfect specimen is hard to find; but it *can* be found, and is well worth the infinite patience, persistence, determination and abnegation necessary for the hunting of it.

I have held many discussions with friends and others about this policy of perfection. The usual argument they have to offer is that the great museums contain many damaged and mended pieces,— and therefore why should a collector of modest means and attainment turn up his nose at a jug with its handle glued back into place?

My reply is that it is quite proper that museums should contain pieces which have been repaired and restored. You will always find, however, that such objects are important specimens; almost invariably they are unique examples; otherwise they certainly would not find a place in the museum. It is because they are the most perfect pieces of their kind obtainable, or even in existence, that they are thus preserved, even though they be spoiled of their original glory.

But a private collector is not an educational institution. It is not his province to preserve for posterity typical examples of a bygone fictile art. I will qualify this generalization by conceding that a private collector of great wealth, such as was Mr. Morgan for instance, is always justified in acquiring unique specimens worthy of preservation, whether damaged or not; for, after all, it is usually the wealthy collector's intention eventually to bequeath or donate his collection to a museum, where it shall be maintained for the benefit and pleasure of posterity. So far as cracked and mended pottery is concerned, therefore, I class Mr. Morgan with the British Museum and the Metropolitan Museum of Art.

But the average collector, your friend and mine, who is interested in china or glass or pewter or prints, should not accumulate imperfect specimens. He should not connive at their preservation.

KING JAMES II AND MARY
OF MODENA

Earthenware dishes decorated in yellow and blue with
portraits of James II (1685-1689) and his consort.
Diameter, 18 inches.   Bristol, 1685.

Victoria and Albert Museum

By refusing to purchase damaged or mended pieces, which are not unique or even rare, but which are obtainable perhaps at a slightly lower price than a perfect specimen of exactly the same thing, collectors would soon discourage dealers from offering this rubbish for sale. But by paying first rate prices for second rate specimens, they merely encourage the dealers to put a premium on junk. The practice of preserving cracked teapots may contribute somewhat to the prosperity of the cement industry, but never will it enrich the store of the world's treasures of art.

Furthermore, the money spent on the purchase of two or three cracked specimens would be put to far better use if expended on the acquisition of a single perfect piece.

The Schreiber Collection, which was formed by Lady Constance Schreiber, and now holds the place of honor in the ceramic section of the Victoria and Albert Museum at South Kensington, occupying several large halls and containing nearly two thousand pieces, is probably the largest and most comprehensive collection of china ever gathered by the personal effort and taste of a single individual. I have spent many hours among its cases, and I cannot recall seeing a single broken or mended piece. No doubt there are some slightly defective pieces, and a few unique and priceless pieces that have been skilfully restored. What I mean to convey, however, is that the condition of perfection is so general that the impression left upon even a careful and close observer

17

is one of unsurpassed beauty and freshness. This, I believe, is the ideal toward which even the most modest collector should aspire.

Adherence to a principle, or an ideal, frequently brings its own reward. Not so often as it might, alas, but perhaps just often enough to convince honest folk that honesty is the best policy. A dealer in Chiswick once offered me a little Sunderland jug at a surprisingly low price, especially as the piece was absolutely perfect and bore one of the rare inscriptions. I knew that such a jug should cost at least three or four times what he was asking for this one. I was suspicious, of course, at once; and as the shop was a small one, cluttered up with all sorts of junk and comparatively few objects of any real value or interest, my first thought was that I had stumbled into a fence. There was little else about the wares in sight, however, to substantiate this theory, and I soon concluded that either the jug was a fake and the dealer knew it, or it was genuine and the dealer did not appreciate its value. I examined it very carefully, and to me it seemed perfectly "right." I decided to take a chance, for it was a very lovely little pot, both in color and texture. I bought it, and as the man was wrapping it up for me I said:

"How is it that you happen to sell this Sunderland jug at so reasonable a figure? The prices on your other things don't seem to me to be as low as this."

"Well," smiled the dealer, cunningly, "I did not pay much for that jug. So I just put a price on it,

18

and anyone can take it or leave it. I don't guarantee anything."

"You mean you don't think it is a right one?" I suggested.

"You did not ask if it was right before you bought it," he retorted. "You certainly took your time about examining it. If you're satisfied, I am."

"I'm satisfied," I said, and then, to draw him out: "I don't care whether it is right or not; it is a fine little jug; good color, good shape, and not a nick or a crack."

"That's just it," admitted the dealer, smugly. "It looks too new. I think it is a wrong one, if you want to know the truth. But as you don't care, what's the difference. I've never seen a jug like that in such perfect condition, so I expect it is a fake. If I thought it was right, I would not sell it to you under two guineas."

I confess my confidence was a trifle shaken by the calm assurance of the late owner of my Sunderland jug; but I consoled myself with the thought that he did not appear to be a particularly cultured person, and that if the jug were indeed a fake, it was an exceedingly clever fake, and I need not feel unduly chagrined at having been fooled.

A few days later I showed it to a gentleman whose judgment of a piece of pottery carries as much weight as a mark burned into the clay, and he assured me that the piece was quite genuine, and of the period I had believed it to be. In fact he was quite enthusi-

19

astic over my little stroke of good luck, and assured me he would like to own the jug himself.

One is not likely nowadays, however, to find any very valuable or unusual piece in the junk shop type of antique store, or in the side street establishments of small dealers. Collectors of china, glass, furniture, prints, etc., have so increased in number that they have more or less educated these dealers to a superficial knowledge of values. Thus, if by chance a junkman or a small dealer acquires a piece which he thinks has some worth, he does not keep it in stock until an appreciative customer drops in to purchase it. He makes a quicker turnover. He takes it to a large dealer and disposes of it at the best bargain he can strike.

The larger antique dealers obtain much of their stock in this way, as well as by frequent tours of inspection among the small and out of the way shops. Indeed, the little fellows, with the assumption of a sort of professional complacency, quite frequently explain their lack of desirable objects by saying that they "have just sold a splendid lot to a dealer."

With the cussedness of all human nature, however, there are some among the lesser shopkeepers, who will positively not sell to other dealers. I have noticed this in England more than elsewhere. Quite frequently, when rummaging about a shop, have I been asked if I were a dealer. I always deny the allegation very promptly, and even make an assiduous effort to establish my amateur standing, for that question is probably never asked except by those to whom dealer customers are unwelcome.

I remember a crabbed old gentleman, the owner of a small shop in Epsom, hobbling toward me out of his cavernous retreat, as I inspected the wares that cluttered the doorway I had just entered,—announced by the usual tinkling of a bell.

"May I look about and see what you have?" I inquired, politely.

"Are you a dealer?" he retorted rather gruffly, glaring at me through a pair of rusty spectacles.

"No, I am not a dealer. If I said I was, would you give me a discount?"

"No," he roared; "I'd show you the door!"

Every now and then, in England, I came across a disagreeable old codger such as this dealer of Epsom. At first I was quite astonished at such an attitude from a merchant toward a possible customer,—for on occasions the manner and words of these strange individuals were thoroughly insulting.

I once discussed this with the amiable lady whose shop is in Baker Street. Her wares were always marked in plain figures, and at pretty stiff prices. At one of my first visits to her shop, when I asked her if ten shillings was not a bit steep for the small object I coveted, she replied:

"Oh, yes; *you* can have it for six!"

I bought it for six shillings, knowing perfectly well that the reduction had not been made because the lady liked the color of my hair, or my *beaux yeux,* as the French have it.

Not long afterwards, when we became better acquainted, I asked her why she marked her pieces at one figure and invariably let me have them for a lesser amount. I pointed out that this was a clumsy sort of flattery which might succeed with the very casual and occasional visitor, but was wholly wasted on hard-boiled antiquers such as most of her customers must be.

"Oh," she explained, "I don't do that to flatter anyone. I do it to protect myself against the dealers. You see, a dealer won't pay such high prices; and I won't come down for a dealer. If he wants the piece, he must pay the marked price. Some of them do, sometimes, and then I feel such a fool for not having known the thing was worth more! I feel as if I had been swindled. But, if I did not put high prices on my things, these dealers would buy my best pieces as fast as I get them, and I should not have anything attractive left to interest private customers,—and then I should not build up a trade. So, everything I have is marked much higher than what I am willing to sell it for to any private customer."

At first this seemed to me a curious point of view, but upon reflection it is plain that the lady's attitude is quite justified. Her sources of supply are probably among her acquaintances and their friends. She cannot successfully compete with the large dealers at the auctions. She acquires her stock by picking up a

KING WILLIAM III AND
QUEEN MARY

Earthenware dish crudely decorated in blue with
portraits of William and Mary (1689-1702).
Diameter, 9 inches. Bristol Delft, *c.* 1690.

QUEEN ANNE

Oval earthenware placque decorated in blue and white
with a portrait of Queen Anne (1702-1714).
Height, 10 inches. Bristol Delft, *c.* 1702.

Victoria and Albert Museum

few pieces at a time from people who need to dispose of some of their possessions, or who tell her of some suburban cottage where she may find a teaset or some Bristol glass. There are many dealers of this type, and in the aggregate they manage to gather a pretty good quality of material. Sometimes, as is the case with all of us, they have to buy inferior pieces in a lot, in order to obtain the good pieces they desire.

The large dealers are well aware of this condition, and make frequent visits to the small shops, where they purchase the desirable objects, and are under no obligation to buy the inferior pieces.

CHAPTER III

Y experience in hunting the antique, while by no means extensive, has been acquired in various sections of our own country and in several foreign lands. Fate, in the form of Business, required that I live in London, at one time, for nearly two years. During that period antiquing was my great recreation. For another similar period I became an exile in Paris, and there again treasure-hunting was my distraction from sterner cares.

Although I have always envied those possessed of the leisure to wander about the countryside, stopping at farm houses by the way, exploring garrets, discovering repairable Chippendale chairs in woodsheds, and retrievable wrecks of early American dressers in chicken coops, I have never been able to indulge in this delightful sport. My hunting has been almost wholly restricted to the paved ways of city streets. My adventures have, for the most part, not been in the open, but rather in those caves and dark recesses, inhabited by that strange tribe of semi-erudite, listless, unambitious beings who seem to bear no resentment against dust, disorder and decay. I have poked about hundreds of shops, and gossiped with as many dealers.

My observations have led me to the conclusion

that the dealer is pretty much the same kind of an individual all the world over. Either certain peculiarities of temperament influence him to become a dealer; or else the business of handling the "select second-hand" develops specific characteristics and idiosyncrasies. Whichever it may be, there is certainly a distinct type, differing only in language and complexion, whether he be of Quebec, Ragusa, London, Paris or Hoboken.

But it is also true that there are innumerable variations of the type,—from the most amiable, highly educated gentleman and woman—down to the surly, ignorant, dishonest charlatan. Fortunately, one encounters but comparatively few of these. On the other hand, I have had the good fortune of meeting many of the finer type, several of whom I am indeed proud to count among my friends.

Between these two extreme varieties lies a vast group of average intelligence, average competence, average manners and average misinformation.

In England, the dealer is almost invariably an Englishman. He is more intelligent and has a better knowledge of his subject than you will find among his kind in America. Here, our average dealer, in most instances, is but a graduate junkman of Central European antecedents, who has acquired a certain trade patter, and bases his appreciation of values largely upon the newspaper reports of metropolitan auction sales,—than which there can be nothing more unsound or deceptive.

But there is one particular characteristic in which dealers seem to run pretty close to type, a peculiarity which divides them fairly accurately into three groups: those who mark their goods in plain figures; those who use hieroglyphics; those who do not mark the prices at all.

In the shops of high-class dealers you will invariably find that the price at which every object is offered for sale is plainly marked in legible figures upon the label. In such a shop you feel a sense of confidence and security, and it never occurs to you to quibble about the price.

In a great many shops—indeed, in too many—the prices are marked in cabalistic combinations of letters or symbols. It becomes necessary for the visitor to inquire the price of every object that may be of some interest to him. This, in itself, is tiresome and annoying. The practice of marking goods in cipher is one that always seems to indicate a lack of frankness and straightforwardness, and is sure to prejudice many visitors, whose inclination to purchase is dampened by doubt and uncertainty as to the accurate interpretation of the symbols. The impression created by this method is that the dealer must be actuated by some ulterior motive, when he chooses to conceal rather than to reveal the true prices at which his wares are for sale. In all such shops it is not only proper, but advisable, to bargain for lower figures than those quoted, and in nine cases out of ten a reduction results. I have never yet been

26

A. C. Cooper

KING GEORGE II

Saltglaze earthenware equestrian figure, 9¼ inches high, ascribed to Astbury, representing King George II (1727-1760), wearing the Order of the Garter and mounted on his charger, directing his troops at the battle of Dettingen, fought on June 27th, 1743, when the combined English and Austrian forces defeated the French under the Duc de Noailles. In memory of this victory, Handel composed his Dettingen Te Deum.

From the Collection of Malcolm Stoner, Esq.

given by any shopkeeper any reason, consistent with business ethics, for marking his retail prices in hieroglyphics.

The third and lowest class of shop is the one where no prices are marked at all. This may be an indication of laziness. Yet, in such places, one may justly suspect any quotation, and properly offer to purchase at whatever sum one's personal judgment or inclination may appraise the object desired.

In junk shops no reasonable man would expect to find every article marked with its price. No junk-man has the leisure or inclination for such efficient salesmanship. Nor is it necessary. A junk shop is a bazaar for bartering, and there,—*caveat emptor*. My feeling is that this motto applies to any shop where prices are not marked in plain figures.

I am willing to make one exception to this generalization, and that is in favor of the gentlewoman who, by stress of circumstances, has embarked in the antique business in preference perhaps to giving piano lessons or writing for the magazines. She may have some slight excuse, at the outset, for not marking her goods. She may not know their value; she probably overestimates them all. She wants to feel her way. But, later on, as she increases her stock by purchase, she has no excuse whatever for not meeting the accepted standards of high-class business. I feel sure, if a census were taken, it would be found that all the amateur lady antique dealers, who fail every year, likewise failed at the start to price-mark their goods; I am also convinced that every one of these worthy ladies, who has made a success in the trade, as many of them have, started out by letting their prospective clients know in plain figures the price at which every object offered could be purchased.

I remember a rather pleasant adventure which I had in a shop in the King's Road, London, where there were no prices marked and where one felt, on entering, that the dealer was of the type to demand whatever he thought the traffic would bear.

In the back of the shop, on a shelf with a lot of miscellaneous rubbish, I noticed what appeared to be a Lambeth stoneware flask, so grimy with dust that I feared at first the piece had been in some way damaged by fire or stain. With a piece of crumpled newspaper I managed to remove enough of the surface crust to make certain that nothing but removable dirt was disfiguring an otherwise undamaged statuette flask of Queen Victoria. It was the piece made just after her coronation, by Doulton & Watts at Lambeth in 1838, picturing the young queen holding in her hand a scroll inscribed "My hope is in my people."

The dealer, attracted by the noise of the crumpled newspaper, as I furbished Queen Victoria's anatomy, came over to me.

"How much for this flask?" I asked.

"Twenty-five shillings," he replied, with considered deliberation.

"Too much," I retorted. "It would take twenty-five shillings of anybody's time to get the dirt off of it."

"But it's a good piece," argued the dealer, relieving me of the Queen, and applying friction with his coat sleeve. "If I had the other one of this pair, I could sell the two for ten pounds."

I smiled rather incredulously.

"I have a customer," he continued, unabashed, "who collects these Lambeth flasks. But he only wants them in pairs. He said any time I could find Prince Albert, the mate to this one, he'd pay ten pounds for the pair."

"I wish you the best of luck," I observed with self-restraint, as I took my leave.

Now it happened that I knew where Prince Albert was. At least I thought I knew where I could lay my hands on the Lambeth flask mate to this dealer's Victoria. For, a few days before, I had made one of my occasional visits to the little shop in Baker Street where I frequently found pieces to my liking. The amiable lady had then chided me for letting so many weeks pass without calling to see her.

"I had such a nice Lambeth flask," she said, reproachfully, "You would have liked it."

"Of course I should have liked it," I exclaimed. "Why did not you keep it for me? You might have sent me a postcard."

"I was keeping it for you," she assured me; "but

a dealer came in and saw it and bought it. She is a friend of mine; I could not very well refuse her."

"And the flask," I inquired, "who was it?" for the lady knew that I was only interested in portrait pieces.

"Albert," she replied, "and such a lovely one!"

"How much was he?" I inquired, rather peevishly.

"Sixteen shillings."

"Sixteen shillings for a Lambeth flask," I exclaimed, with all the dramatic horror I could assume.

"But Albert is being collected now," the lady replied, almost reprovingly, as if that were sufficient explanation for any fancy price. As a matter of fact, for a clean, undamaged specimen, the price was just about right. I was extremely annoyed at having missed the opportunity by a few days.

"Where is this dealer who has him now?" I inquired presently.

"In Hampton Court,—right near the Palace."

Horrors! Just where hundreds of tourists were sure to see Albert every day. I had a sinking feeling that he must already have been captured. I decided to go to Hampton Court the very next morning. Then I had a better thought.

"Could not you buy him back?" I asked. "How much do you suppose she wants for him?"

"Probably a guinea. I'll have a try for you, if you like!"

"Please do," I urged. "A guinea,—even a little more." And I went out into the rain of Baker Street,

FREDERICK, DUKE OF YORK

Elaborately decorated and inscribed earthenware bowl showing an equestrian portrait of the second son of King George III. Diameter, 9 inches. Height, 3¾ inches. Liverpool. *c.* 1790.

FREDERICK WILLIAM I, KING OF PRUSSIA

Earthenware dish with edge modelled in low relief, inscribed and decorated in color with a posthumous portrait of the father of Frederick the Great, King of Prussia. Diameter, 17 inches. Staffordshire ware, decorated in Holland, *c.* 1760.

Schreiber Collection, Victoria and Albert Museum

—quite excited, and wondering if, after all, I ought not to repair immediately to Hampton Court myself. But it was closing time, and dark and cold and wet; so I went home instead.

It is only natural, therefore, that I should have been quite thrilled when I came upon Victoria in the King's Road shop and heard the dealer's assertion that an anonymous collector was willing to pay ten pounds for such a pair. To be sure, I was very doubtful of the existence of this anonymous collector of Lambeth ware. Almost every dealer has a mythical customer who will always surely buy the piece you are looking at. It was because I did not believe in the imaginary customer, with ten pounds to spend, that I felt safe in leaving Victoria where she was. I felt quite confident that, barring the worst kind of luck, she would still be available a few days hence, and probably at a different quotation. And I was not mistaken. The lady of Baker Street recaptured Albert for me, and, with half the pair safe in my cabinet, I set out again for the King's Road, to purchase Victoria. I retrieved her from the darkness of the back shop and rubbed off a little more of the grime. I had a faint hope that the dealer might not remember me.

"How much for this?" I asked, as nonchalantly as I could.

"Same as I told you last week," he replied.

"Well, what was that?" I queried, innocently, as

31

if the original discussion about the price had entirely faded from my memory.

"Twelve and six," he said.

I derived almost as much satisfaction out of the verification of my price-marking theory as I did at the decrease of fifty per cent in the price of the Queen.

But, when I got her home, and had scrubbed her and polished her, and set her up on the mantelpiece, alongside of Albert, I became fully aware of what I should have realized before,—that this particular Victorian piece was not one of a pair at all, and that my Albert, at least in a ceramic sense, was not her mate. Albert had his name moulded in raised letters across the front of the round base on which he stood. Victoria's base bore no lettering. Furthermore, this Lambeth Victoria, with her scroll in her hand, was of an earlier period, if only by a few years, than the Albert flask. It represented the young Queen making her first address from the throne, when she had said that her hope was in her people. She had not yet married the Prince Consort; otherwise she might have said that her hope was in Albert.

So, of course, there could not be a pair in this case,—which was additional evidence of the King's Road dealer's mendacity concerning the astute collector who would buy the Queen if he could procure the other one of the pair.

Now, however, I found myself somewhat in the position of the mythical collector. I must find the

Victoria to match my Albert,—for I knew *he* certainly was one of a Lambeth pair. Indeed, I had seen and coveted such a pair in the London Museum. It took me two years, though, to achieve my purpose. But one day I did obtain the Victorian mate to my Albert, at an auction, and I had to take three other pieces I did not really want, because my Victoria was included in a "lot."

The terminology of antiquing is not so precise as it might be. It is perhaps more accurate to say that antiquers are not always precise in the use of their vocabulary. Take this word "pair" for instance. The average dealer, and most writers of auction catalogues, seem to make no distinction between "pair" and "two." In many shops, and at many sales, I have seen two examples of exactly the same piece labeled and priced as a pair. This is one respect in which pottery differs from poker. Two spaniels facing to the left are not a pair. To be a "pair" the objects must face each other, or balance each other in composition, or be a male and a female. The dictionary definition of pair is quite unsatisfactory: "Two things accompanying each other in the use intended; as a pair of shoes, gloves, etc."

This may be fair enough, as definitions go, but it fails to apply accurately or completely to a pair of ceramic ornaments. These should obviously "accompany each other in the use intended"; but they must have other characteristics besides. They must not only "accompany each other," but they must conform to "the use intended" in the well balanced decoration of a shelf or mantelpiece, or the top of a chest of drawers. Obviously, therefore, the objects may not both be exactly alike. One must face to the left and the other to the right. This does not mean that they should be profiles; it means that the position of one figure, or the composition of one group, must, in attitude and design, balance harmoniously with the other.

Two vases are not a pair if exactly alike in form and color. They are merely two of a kind, one of which may easily be replaced in case of breakage. A real "pair" of vases consists of two vessels similarly modeled and colored, but differently decorated with complementary or balancing designs. With vases, or urns, the form may be identical; the basic colors should be identical; but the distinctive decorations, whether they be relief designs or pictorial medallions, must be apposite.

There is, of course, the exception that proves the rule. There are two pottery objects, which come in pairs, that are usually, although not necessarily, exactly alike. These are birdseed holders and furniture rests. The former are usually in the form of busts, sometimes portraits, sometimes not, or animals' heads, or flowers, or castles. They have a projection at the back which was inserted between the wire bars of the birdcages of the Chinese style that were so popular in the Georgian period. These projections are hollow and have an orifice at the inner

34

end on the upper side, for the birdseed. There were always two of these birdseed holders, one to be placed at each end, or on each side, of the cage,— and consequently they were sold in pairs.

The same reason for duplication applied to furniture rests. These are heavy earthenware supports for the two front legs of chests. At first they bore no decoration; but in the late Eighteenth Century they were made in the form of human heads, or lions' heads, etc. Infrequently they come in dissimilar pairs, —as the heads of a man and a woman. Usually they are exactly alike, lest they appear to be a disassorted makeshift. Portraits occur occasionally, the most commonly to be found being the head of Princess Charlotte, daughter of George IV.

While on the subject of terminology, it may not be out of place to touch here upon the use and misuse of the word "china," as applied to ceramic products. As we are all well aware, the word "china," in its ceramic sense, is an abbreviation for "chinaware,"— a term which came into general use in England toward the middle of the Seventeenth Century upon the introduction of tea from the East. It was tea, and tea drinking, which introduced porcelain to western civilization. Until the first importation of tea, a considerable portion of the population of England drank beer or ale for breakfast, as well as at social gatherings later in the day. In the northern parts, broth was occasionally taken in the morning, just as soup was taken by the peasants of France,—

and still is. No lighter morning beverage was known, for, like tea, neither coffee nor chocolate had yet been acquired from the far lands overseas.

Thus, when tea was discovered, so to speak, dainty vessels suitable for serving it had to be supplied. These, too, were brought from China, by the same ships that carried the chests of tea; and as, at that time, no English pottery produced any ceramics more delicate than stoneware jugs and platters, there was immediately inaugurated a brisk trade in what was termed "China-ware."

Thus started the confusion which has persisted, more or less, until the present day. For, with the general use of chinaware, the word china fell into popular use for the designation of the lighter forms of pottery, whether these were of porcelain or earthenware. It is therefore not surprising that the novice in the study of ceramic art, and the dilettante in china collecting, are always more or less puzzled by the seeming confusion, the almost synonymous use of the terms employed to indicate the two great divisions of the potter's product,—porcelain and earthenware. It generally takes a long time for them to understand clearly the difference between the two; to know which, if either, may properly be called "china"; and to use the word "pottery" in its correct sense. But they need not feel discouraged or downcast, for it is largely due to the careless and inaccurate use of these ceramic terms, by writers on the subject, that most people speak of "china" without knowing

KING GEORGE III

Earthenware bust, ascribed to Enoch Wood.   Staffordshire, c. 1790.
Height, 12¼ inches.

Victoria and Albert Museum

whether they mean porcelain or earthenware, or both.

The dictionaries define pottery as "objects of clay molded into form while in a moist and plastic condition, and then hardened by fire." Thus the term "pottery" embraces both porcelain and earthenware, and even includes stoneware, the harder, coarser product which we associate with cider jugs and cookie jars. Porcelain is translucent. Earthenware is opaque. China is synonymous with porcelain. It is therefore correct to use the word china when referring to porcelain, although the general public have for long adopted the word as a generic term, meaning any kind of glazed ceramic object, with the possible exception of stoneware. To the average person, a Staffordshire earthenware dog is a "china figure," and a Chelsea porcelain shepherdess is also a "china figure."

"Pottery" is colloquially used in the sense of "earthenware," generally with reference to the coarser varieties of clay products. This is incorrect, because the finest piece of *famille verte,* or the daintiest Dresden group, as well as the lowliest flowerpot or drain-pipe, are all pottery.

Mrs. Earle's book on *China Collecting in America* treats much more of earthenware than of porcelain. Dr. Barber's *Old English China with American Views* records, describes and catalogues the old blue Staffordshire earthenware, and gives but little space

37

to porcelain. In the letter-press of their books both of these authors use the word "china" as a generic term for all ceramic wares. While this may be technically inaccurate, common usage has given to "china" an inclusive meaning embracing all of the glazed products of wheel and kiln.

CHAPTER IV

OR several years after my acquisitive instinct first prompted me to acquire one or two insignificant pieces of pottery, I had little leisure or means or opportunity to indulge in the luxury of collecting; for just as "opportunity makes the thief," so, to a great extent, opportunity likewise makes the collector. But during all this time my dormant interest in pottery always rose at the chance of visiting a museum or, from time to time, the exhibition of some great collection about to be offered for sale. And so it happened that one day, in the Metropolitan Museum, I saw, in a loan of a collection of Frankliniana, a Staffordshire toby-jug alleged to represent Benjamin Franklin. It stood in a case with other porcelains, medals, prints, etc., associated in various ways, but mostly as to portraiture, with the sage of Philadelphia. It was a quaint and attractive piece. I think it was the first portrait toby-jug I had ever seen. It fascinated me. I pondered that, no doubt, other famous figures had been made into tobies. The desire was there and then born in me to acquire, some day, such of these pottery portraits as good fortune might place in my path.

Now, whether the germ implanted that day spurred my power of observation, or whether it was coincidence, or fate, or fortune, or whatever you choose to call it,——chance, if you like,——the fact remains that not many weeks later, in an obscure New York side street, in the cluttered window of a second-hand shop, I discovered a duplicate of this Benjamin Franklin toby-jug.

I gazed long and steadily from the pavement, and finally went into the shop. This was a good many years ago; I had had no experience in antiquing. I feared to let the shopkeeper know of my interest in the jug. I talked about brass candlesticks, and pewter dishes, and other objects; and finally picked up the toby, in which apparently the dealer had no interest whatever, for he offered it at a ridiculously low price.

When I got home and had carefully washed my treasure, and set him up in a position of honor and vantage, I sat and gazed long and admiringly upon him. There is a subtile charm about pottery, a certain fascination of frailty; an appeal which is not offered by silver or copper or even by painted canvas. When you take up a piece of chinaware, you handle it fondly; you almost coddle it; for baked clay must rest confidingly in your grasp lest it fall and be destroyed. There is almost genuine dependence about pottery which promotes a pride of ownership, a sense of responsibility,——almost a sense of duty.

It was this glamor that I began to feel with my first toby. I pictured other tobies grouped about him, on shelves and in cabinets, and dreamed those dreams which every enthusiast has dreamed at the incipiency of that harmless form of insanity which, after all, has been the reason for the preservation to this world of many of our greatest works of art.

It was unquestionably this Franklin toby which lent direction to my taste, and inspired me with the desire to acquire other tobies that should be the portraits of famous folk. Thereafter I began reading up my subject in the library of an occasional afternoon; and I took long walks in odd quarters of the city, in the hope of spying out other jugs of a similar kind. But New York, at that period, was not an especially fertile field for the acquisition of toby-jugs. It was months before I came across another; but I got just as much of a thrill then as I had out of Mr. Franklin.

My second jug, like the first, was a Staffordshire piece, of about 1860, representing Gladstone, sitting, leaning against a tree-trunk with an axe resting between his knees. Here was a gentle cartooning of the great statesman's eugenic practice, in his later years, of cutting down a tree every morning before breakfast.

It was in the latter part of the Eighteenth Century that the toby-jug was adapted not only to friendly cartoon, but to a convivial quality of hero-worship. Great men's faces were fitted to jugs just as, nowadays, the likenesses of our national characters are cast in plaster of Paris, and sold in the shops. So it is that we find Napoleon and Wellington, Nelson and Drake, hollowed into ale mugs for the greater glory of their deeds. It has even been asserted that here

41

originated the unhandsome term "mug," as the col-
loquial designation for face.

From the collector's viewpoint, there are two
classes of toby-jugs,—the portrait-jug, and the face-
jug which is merely a comic. The portraits may be
of historical personages such as Napoleon or Nelson;
or they may simulate fictitious beings such as John
Bull and Punch; or they may represent characters
from romance and the drama, such as Falstaff or
Uncle Toby, who endowed with his name this vast
tribe of personalized pots, of the number and variety
of which no man has yet made full record.

For the name "Toby" is generally supposed to
have been adopted from Sterne's jovial character of
Uncle Toby in *Tristram Shandy,*—the little squat
jug having come into popular favor at about the
time people were first reading Sterne's novel, in
1759. On the other hand, it is fairly well established
that Whieldon made jugs of this type,—seated figures
holding pipe and mug,—decorated with the typical
Whieldon mottling. It seems perhaps more probable
that the name "Toby" was an Eighteenth Century
colloquialism, the accepted designation of those with
convivial inclinations, and that Sterne adopted the
name for his character, just as Dickens later chose
many names which defined and personified his fictional creations, either by their phonetic sound or by
the meaning of the word itself in its original sense.

The theory that Toby is a folk-lore name, a word
that found its way into the language from the tap-

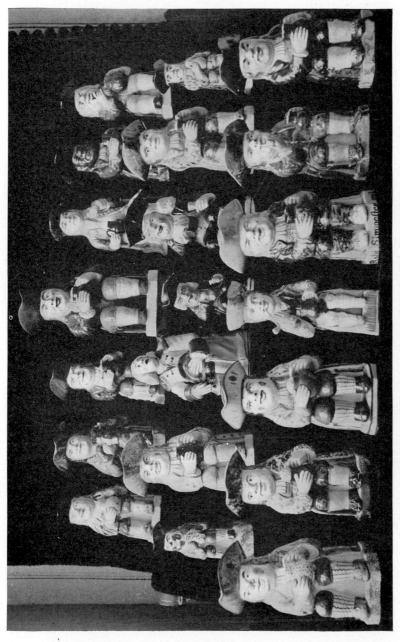

GROUP OF EIGHTEENTH AND NINETEENTH CENTURY TOBY-JUGS

From the Collection of G. W. Horsfield, Esq.

room and the tavern, rather than from the creative brain of a novelist, is somewhat supported by the fact that there is an old English ballad (which, so far, I have been unable to trace in its entirety) that relates at considerable length the unfortunate fate which befell poor Toby's remains. It seems that his unctuous clay was found particularly suitable for pottery purposes, and that some imaginative potter fashioned it into a jug, representing his person and bearing his name. This, the ballad tells us, was the parent of all similar jugs. Equally unfortunate apparently was Toby's wife, Agnes, in failing to secure undisturbed rest. Her story is told on a jug in the Willett Collection, at Brighton, and the first two lines, no doubt, refer to the old Toby ballad:

> Toby's fame, like his size, spread so great by his ale
> That for Agnes no room could be found in the tale.
> Now the potter who shrewdly found Toby's remains
> Thought a visit again there might answer his pains
> And he read on a tomb, void of sorrow and care:
> "The wife of old Toby, fair Agnes, lies here."
> At these lines our shrewd potter a happy thought started
> That Toby and Agnes should never be parted.
> So he took her fair clay which was whiter than milk
> And tempered with brandy till softer than silk;
> Then formed into pipes he advised, sly and snug,
> That we kiss her fair clay and shake hands with his jug.

Thus, according to the early balladists, the clay of Toby was moulded into jugs, and the milky, silky clay of Agnes, his wife, was fashioned into pipes, that she might not be separated from her spouse so long as convivial souls gather together in this world.

But other face-jugs and man-jugs were made long before the English potters idealized Uncle Toby, and these were based on the same idea of tavern cartoon and caricature that has been so elaborately developed in the tobies. As far back as there are any examples to show, the Flemish and German stoneware beer pots used to be decorated at the top of the neck with a rough design resembling a man's bearded face. Hence the names "graybeards" and "longbeards" applied to this type of jug. It was not until about the middle of the Seventeenth Century, however, that these jugs assumed any identity,— when they became generally designated as Bellarmines.

The Flemish potters were for the most part adherents to the reformed religion which had been cruelly suppressed and persecuted by Cardinal Bellarmine, the Pope's representative in the Netherlands. Thus, at the Cardinal's death, there was no regret or mourning on the part of the potters who, on the contrary, sought to express their scorn and hatred of their late enemy by putting his face on common beer pots, that his memory might be perpetuated by ribald jest in the ale-houses. So universal did this practice become in the Low Countries, that Bellarmine soon became the accepted designation for an ale jug; and by that name are these vessels still known.

And even earlier than the time of the detested Cardinal, away back in the days of the Incas, the man-jugs, or huacos, or portrait-jars of Peru were common pottery. There is an extensive collection of them to be seen in the American Museum of Natural History, in New York. There can be no doubt that each of these huacos was intended as a portrait of some Peruvian worthy. The theory is that the jars, frequently found in tombs, were intended to provide liquid sustenance for the departed on his journey to the other world. But this is perhaps mere speculation on the part of learned ethnologists. Who knows but that the huacos were made in the same spirit of cartoon as were the Bellarmines and the tobies? It is pleasanter, for me at least, to think that perhaps they were; and to associate with these quaint and very human looking vessels a more cheerful reason for existence than has been generally ascribed to them.

And yet, even if the huacos did add to the gaiety of Peruvian inns, at about 1000 A.D., it would scarcely be reasonable to infer that they were of any direct ancestry to our toby-jugs. The probability is that, since the great beginning, all races have at times carved faces on their pouring or drinking vessels. The Egyptians did, the Mexicans did; and even in darkest Africa, now that negroid art is being studied, we find tankards of wood and of ivory ornamented with extremely terrifying countenances. And yet, while we may appreciate that the type of face-jug is of a remote ancestry, we may still rejoice in its development into toby form, and award to the

Staffordshire potters the honor of having introduced art into the taproom. They surely deserve our gratitude for having lent a certain grace to a homely vessel; for having added sentimental associations to the commonplace act of pouring beer out of a pitcher.

At first, the toby was a gaily colored jug in the form of a man, seated, holding a pipe or an ale mug in his hand. He always wore a cocked hat, because the tricorn furnished the ideal shape for the pitcher's lip. In the earliest examples there was no attempt at individual portraiture, although in many cases, the figures were to a certain extent designed to represent a type other than Uncle Toby, and many bore names such as the Jolly Good Fellow, the Post-boy, the Snuff Taker and the Night Watchman. The latter is frequently mistaken for Dr. Johnson, and in imitations, is usually miscolored.

When variety came into demand, Toby was cast in a great diversity of countenance. Some of him, the Jolly Good Fellow and the Snuff Taker for instance, were made full length. It soon occurred to some individual of commercial instinct that a portrait of the King might prove salable, and there is a Nottingham jug alleged to be a portrait of George II. This toby shows a greedy-eyed, hawk-nosed, heavy-jowled, bloated countenance, bearing considerable resemblance to the King in the later years of his life. But it is a cruel caricature, and would suggest even to those least familiar with English history, that

46

BELLARMINE JUG

Saltglazed stoneware. Height, 14 inches,
made in Bouffloux, Belgium, c. 1700.

Pennsylvania Museum of Art

J. H. Hare

PERUVIAN HUACOS, OR PORTRAIT JARS

Red clay modeled and decorated with colored pigments, made in Peru about the Tenth
Century, A. D. The tallest of these three jars is 11 inches high. (See page 45.)

Gaffron Collection, American Museum of Natural History

George II was not especially popular with the tavern folk of his day.

From the point of view of craftsmanship, the Eighteenth Century toby-jugs are far superior in modeling, and more interesting in color and glaze, than those of a later period. They bring high prices, both at auction, and at private sale. Obtainable good specimens of the genuine article are scarce. Fraudulent imitations have been sold to a considerable extent; but the fakes can never really approximate the tone values and the soft glazes of the original pieces.

Few portrait tobies were made by the Eighteenth Century potters, but, to the toby collector, this is of little or no moment, as his interest is in pottery, not portraiture. My own interest in toby-jugs, on the contrary, has always been in their qualities of portraiture, this being perhaps due to the fact that the first such jug to come into my possession was an alleged portrait of Benjamin Franklin. I have since determined that it is not a portrait of Franklin, and never was intended as such, in spite of the fact that its replica was so designated in the collection of Frankliniana that I saw years ago in the Metropolitan Museum.

I have seen this same piece, a Staffordshire product of about 1850, offered in two auction sales within the past ten years. In one case it was catalogued as Benjamin Franklin, and in the second case it was correctly described as a likeness of Mr. Pickwick. A cursory examination of the figure's costume will immediately convince any observer that the potter intended to portray Mr. Pickwick and not Benjamin Franklin. The squat little figure wears tight white trousers tucked into gaiters, a manner of dress quite foreign to Franklin's time or habit. There is no facial likeness to Franklin, and none of that statesman's dignity is reflected in the attitude or pose of the figure. His spectacles have fallen forward upon the end of his nose, and he looks out over them benignly and undisturbed. I could wish the jug were a portrait of Franklin, but it unquestionably is not; and there is no profit in self-deception.

It was not until late in the Eighteenth and early in the Nineteenth Centuries that the Staffordshire potters began extensively to encourage or cater to hero-worship by more or less decorously moulding the features of their nation's worthies into tavern-ware.

Napoleon, Nelson and Wellington were probably the most tobied of any public characters—not only in England, but in France as well, and later, even in America. Wellington toby-jugs and face-jugs were made at many places in Staffordshire, at Lambeth and at Rockingham. The Rockingham Wellington toby was copied in the 1850's at Bennington, probably by making a mould from an English Rockingham jug. Mr. John Spargo has established the fact that such jugs were actually produced in Vermont; but as the Bennington "Rockingham" so closely resembles the original English ware, it would be extremely difficult for the most expert today to differentiate between the English and the American product.

On the occasion of the Centenary of the Battle of Waterloo, in 1915, the Copelands, successors of Spode, at Stoke-on-Trent, produced a beautiful figure-jug in porcelain, modeled by Owen Hale, A.R.A. The Duke is represented seated, clad in the full regalia of a field marshal, with cocked and feathered hat, red cape, thrown back to display the decorations on his chest. He wears the characteristic Wellington boots; in his left hand he clasps his great cavalry sword, and in his right his field marshal's baton. The face is excellently modeled and colored,—an accurate and impressive portrait. It appears that only six copies of this piece were made, two of which have come to America.

Nelson jugs are equally numerous, the one most often seen being the standing figure of the Admiral, with the empty sleeve across his chest. This was originally produced in Staffordshire in the early Nineteenth Century, and the first specimens were made of a high grade of earthenware, carefully colored, and covered with a fine quality of lead glaze. Many reproductions of this figure have been made ever since, even by the Staffordshire potters themselves, for they have developed an excellent eye for business. But the later specimens are poorly and often carelessly colored, the clay is of a coarser grade

49

and the glaze of a vastly inferior quality. The recent are quite easily distinguishable from the early products.

Another Staffordshire Nelson portrait-jug of early Nineteenth Century make presents a striking portrait of the British naval hero. The general color effect of the piece is white, with a fine deep glaze. The only color is on the hat, which is blue with a red and gold cockade, and on the broad red sash, which crosses his breast from the right shoulder to the waist. Nelson's proudly cherished decorations,— his "four stars,"—are in gold, one having a red centre. (These four stars were the Order of the Bath, St. Ferdinand and Merit, the Crescent, and St. Joachim. It was customary in his time for Knights always to wear their orders, and Nelson never appeared without his. They were the indirect cause of his death.) From his neck hang two circular medals, the upper one decorated with a ship, the lower one inscribed "Nile 1793." The epaulets and the piping of the uniform are penciled in gold, as is the cuff of the empty right sleeve which is pinned across the breast. The bust rests on a circular base which forms the bottom of the jug.

At Lambeth, about 1820, Doulton & Watts made a similar stoneware portrait-jug of Nelson, which is also excellent as to portraiture. This was produced in three sizes, the largest to hold about two quarts, the smallest being about pint size. Stoneware portrait-jugs, of the toby type, were likewise made of

MR. PICKWICK

A toby-jug frequently miscalled Benjamin Franklin. Height, 7½ inches.
Staffordshire, c. 1860 (See pages 40 and 48.)

J. H. Hare

WILLIAM EWART GLADSTONE

Four times Prime Minister of England. Height, 9¼ inches.
Staffordshire, c. 1880. (See page 41.)

Napoleon by Stephen Green at Lambeth, about 1815.

Some of the English contemporary toby-jugs of Napoleon were caricatures, but most of those made later are honest attempts at portraiture. The French products naturally idealize their hero. In 1876, a Napoleon toby was produced by the Columbia Potteries at Philadelphia,—and I have several times seen this piece described in sales catalogues as "old Staffordshire."

In America the first tobies to be made were probably potted at Bennington. The ordinary little brown toby-jug of the chophouse and the Rockingham portrait toby of Wellington were quite extensively copied and manufactured there. Fenton and Lyman also produced, about 1850, what has since been widely accepted as a Benjamin Franklin toby-jug, although such intention is doubtful. In color this jug is typical of Bennington ware,—brown, mottled with yellow. The genial-faced figure wears the conventional tricorn hat with cockade; his long hair falls over his shoulders; he holds a glass in his right hand, and clasps his cloak about him with his left. The handle of the jug is modeled in the form of a man's trousered leg, the booted foot resting against the back of the hat, the trousers held down under the boot's instep by a strap. Unlike the conventional chophouse toby-jug, which no doubt inspired this model, the Bennington jug flares out to its greatest diameter at the base, being thus almost conical in form.

While this jug has been frequently referred to, and pictured in some books, as a representation of Benjamin Franklin, I am extremely doubtful that the potter ever intended to portray the Quaker sage of Philadelphia, when he modeled it. The features bear no resemblance whatever to Franklin. The figure, like most tobies, is shown holding a glass of ale in one hand, which is wholly out of character with Franklin. Furthermore, while the handle of the jug, being modeled in the form of a man's long trousered leg, is a feature of costume wholly correct as of the period in which the jug was made, it is a ridiculous anachronism in connection with Franklin, who never wore, and probably never saw anyone else wear, long trousers of this fashion. It seems extremely unlikely that a potter, making a portrait of Franklin, would design a handle so out of keeping with his subject.

In the early Nineties, J. S. W. Starkey, a potter of East Liverpool, Ohio, made glazed earthenware portrait-jugs of Washington, William Penn and Pope Leo XIII. These were produced at the East Liverpool Art Pottery,—thirty dozen of Washington, twenty-five dozen of Pope Leo XIII, but only a few of William Penn. The first two jugs are heads only, of excellent portraiture, but the Penn jug is modeled in full figure.

Porcelain tobies of George Washington, in several

sizes, were produced by Lenox, at Trenton, N. J., in 1896. These pieces were modeled by Isaac Broome. The Lenox potteries also produced a William Penn toby, modeled by W. W. Gallimore.

At the time of McKinley's first campaign for the presidency, in 1896, the Bennet Pottery Company, of Baltimore, produced a McKinley toby. It is crude and of inferior quality, bearing very little likeness to McKinley, but it is interesting nevertheless. These tobies were carried in a political parade in Dayton by the employees of the pottery.

Another president, Theodore Roosevelt, was represented in toby form by Lenox, of Trenton, after a design by Edward Penfield, modeled by Broome, who did the Washington toby mentioned above. The jug is of porcelain, and was issued just at the close of Roosevelt's last term of office, when he was about to set forth on his big game hunting expedition into Africa. He is represented in Rough Rider's uniform, his face brightened with the characteristic Roosevelt grin. In his left hand he holds a gun; in his right he clasps a red guide-book, inscribed "Africa." The handle of the jug is formed as an elephant's head. The portraiture of Roosevelt is excellent, and the coloring of the piece is correct in every detail.

In 1910, Doulton & Watts, of Lambeth, England, likewise made a portrait-jug of Roosevelt, in brown salt-glazed stoneware.

For the presidential campaign of 1928 the Patriotic Potteries Association of Philadelphia issued jugs modeled with the faces of President Hoover and Governor Smith. They are of a uniform white in color, and were produced in porcelain by the Onandaga Pottery Company, of Syracuse, N. Y., and in earthenware by the Owen China Company, of Minerva, Ohio. Twenty-five thousand of each candidate were made in porcelain, and seven thousand in earthenware.

In England, few toby-jugs were made during the latter part of the Nineteenth Century, but after the Great War there came a renascence of interest in this form of ceramic art. Admiral Beatty was tobified in several designs. A series of eleven portrait toby-jugs, designed by Sir F. Carruthers Gould, modeled by A. J. Wilkinson, was produced in 1918 at the Royal Staffordshire Pottery, Burslem, for Soane & Smith, of London, and included Lord Kitchener, Field Marshal Sir John French, Marshal Joffre, Admiral Lord Jellicoe, Premier David Lloyd George, Earl Haig, Admiral Beatty, Marshal Foch, General Botha, President Wilson and King George V. Only two hundred and fifty copies were made of the Kitchener jug, and only three hundred and fifty copies of French, Joffre, Jellicoe, Lloyd George, Haig and Beatty. Five hundred each were made of Foch, Botha and Wilson, and one thousand of the King. The moulds were then destroyed. The jugs were sold at two guineas each, when first produced, but the Kitchener is now quoted at twenty-six pounds, and

THEODORE ROOSEVELT

Brightly colored porcelain jug, designed by Edward Penfield, modeled by
Isaac Broome.   Lenox, Trenton, N. J. 1909.

WILLIAM PENN

Porcelain jug, designed and modeled by Isaac Broome. Lenox, Trenton, N. J. 1910.

the others at from three pounds to eight pounds, the King bringing seven guineas.

In 1927 the Ashtead Potters, near Epsom, produced two excellent portrait-jugs of Stanley Baldwin, the British Prime Minister, and of David Lloyd George, from designs by Percy Metcalfe. They are of earthenware, of a uniform cream white color, very well modeled and rather different in shape from the usual portrait-jug. It was from these that the Syracuse modeler of the Hoover and Smith jugs derived his inspiration, following perhaps all too closely the attitude, form and color of the English designs, even to the printed autographs along the base of the pieces.

A toby-jug ten inches high, labeled BENJAMIN FRANKLIN, was also produced by the Ashtead Potters in 1929, from a design by Percy Metcalfe, but it is so clumsily modeled and so crudely colored that it seems hardly possible this could be the work of the same hand that produced the excellent Baldwin and Lloyd George jugs. It bears no resemblance whatever in face or form to Franklin; it is merely a figure of a man seated in an armchair, holding the Liberty Bell on his knees. Perhaps we may rejoice, with the inscription upon its base, that "the edition of these jugs is strictly limited."

CHAPTER V

VERY collector, as he progresses in his search for the particular type of bibelot that has become his hobby, finds his attention constantly distracted and his interest unwillingly aroused in some kindred form of art or craftsmanship. If you are interested in collecting little boxes, you soon begin to take notice of little baskets. If you are looking for miniatures, it is surprising how often you run across charming silhouettes. If you crave teapots, it becomes distressing to discover how many really beautiful coffee pots are obtainable.

This makes it difficult, however strong-minded you may be, however determined to stick to your chosen "line," not to succumb eventually to the temptation of broadening your sphere. At first you resist bravely. You reason that it is futile to attempt to acquire all things that are beautiful, even if they have real value and are bargains. You realize that a modest group of objects of a similar type is far more interesting and attractive than a miscellaneous aggregation of varied character. In the first case, you have a collection, however modest; in the second you have only an assemblage of articles representing nothing more than your good taste in bric-a-brac. It becomes a constant struggle to maintain the narrow path.

After all, a hobby, I suppose, like any other mount, will shy now and then; and it takes a skilled and experienced rider never to be thrown.

In my own case, I soon found that where usually my hunt for tobies failed, I frequently uncovered attractive jugs decorated with transfer printed portraits of notables, or gaily colored earthenware statuettes of an engaging charm. My weakness for portraiture soon rebelled against being confined to toby-jugs,—which, after all, I persuaded myself, must be comparatively limited in number.

And so, from time to time, I succumbed to temptation, and before long, found myself the possessor of a little group of statesmen, military heroes and other worthies,—mostly statuettes from Staffordshire and Rockingham or jugs from Liverpool, Lambeth, Leeds and Sunderland. My complete downfall occurred when I went to live for some two years in London. There I surrendered to the fascination of these quaint bits of pottery, so often did I stumble across figures of recognizable celebrities. Some were not always recognizable, perhaps, by the accuracy of their portraiture, but easily identified either by the inscription on the base, or, where such inscription was lacking, by the action represented in the modeling. I soon realized that my collector's interest was not, indeed, in the mere accumulation of toby-jugs, as such, else on many occasions I should have acquired others than those representing some historical or fictional character. I awoke to the fact that my real weakness was for portraits in pottery, and that these invariably appealed to me, whether in the form of tobies, statuettes, groups, mugs, placques, printed jugs, or even plates. The joys and opportunities of the hunt were immediately vastly broadened and increased.

It would be difficult to state exactly when the first portraits in pottery were made. Doubtless some of the ancient Kiang Hsi figures represent individual mandarins or poets or statesmen who flourished under the Ming dynasty. Nor is it at all unlikely that many of the dainty Tanagra figurines, modeled four centuries before Christ, represent dancers whose fame had spread throughout Bœotia,—for among the statuettes still preserved in our museums, we can identify figures of Mercury, Leda, Bacchus and other demigods. Yet, so far as I am aware, no collection of these early statuettes has ever been based on portraiture. Their interest and value rest rather upon their artistic merit and beauty.

Furthermore, the fictile products of those remote eras have always seemed to me so far beyond the reach of one who might indulge in collecting portraits in pottery merely as an avocation, as an occasional modest pastime, that I have necessarily restricted my own interest to a period much closer to our own times, to one into which I could delve with a greater confidence of assembling a little group of congruous objects,—not one in particular, perhaps, having any great intrinsic value—but which, collec-

Shakespeare   John Locke   Shakespeare   Tennyson   Milton

Walter Scott   Gibbon   Dante   Dr. Johnson   Robert Burns

H. H. Costain

AUTHORS AND POETS

tively, represent a more or less orderly scheme and consistent purpose. And, as most of my opportunities for collecting portrait pieces have been in America and England, my taste inclines rather to the English than to the Continental products, and to earthenware rather than to porcelain. There is a virility and humanness about the coarser product which offers to me a stronger appeal. The porcelain statuettes of Chelsea, Derby, Bow, Meissen and Sèvres are dainty and delicate; but they have always seemed to me somewhat lacking in forcefulness and character. They are feminine, if not effeminate. In England, at least, the strong men have been almost invariably portrayed in earthenware,—the porcelain pieces being mostly of ideal or abstract subjects such as Spring, Harvest, Cupid, Love, Asia, Africa, etc.

Portraits in pottery have been more or less extensively made in most European countries from the middle of the Seventeenth Century. The first efforts were crude placques, medallions and plates; but in the Eighteenth, and particularly in the Nineteenth Century, statuettes and figures reached the highest perfection of ceramic art. In Italy even as early as the Fifteenth Century, the Della Robbias, in Florence, were producing brilliantly enameled terra-cotta bas-reliefs and other sculptures of the highest merit. But these rather massive decorations were mostly of a religious character and hardly come within the scope of our discussion. Later on, the Italian potters produced many smaller figures and statuettes, generally in majolica, and almost invariably representing Madonnas or Saints. The portraiture in these cases is obviously ideal or imaginative, and consequently such pieces bear but a collateral relation to a collection of portrait pieces. Of late years, however, the Florentine potters have produced earthenware busts of Dante, Cellini, and other eminent figures of the Middle Ages; and recently there have appeared several statuettes of Mussolini.

In the beginning, in France, conditions similar to those in Italy prevailed with respect to earthenware figures, these being mostly of religious subjects. But with the development and progress of the porcelain factories, notably at Sèvres, portrait statuettes of rare beauty and high quality were produced from the middle of the Eighteenth Century. The same is true with respect to Germany, where the Saxon factories brought figure-making to the highest excellence, so much so that even today the phrase "a Dresden china shepherdess" is an expression of all that is dainty and refined. The Sèvres and the Saxon factories made, and still make, a great variety of busts and portraits of historical personages, the Sèvres products, however, being mostly in bisque.

It was not until late in the Seventeenth Century that the pottery industry, in England, assumed any noteworthy importance. The earliest form of pottery portraiture as practiced there, was in the decoration of earthenware platters and plates. These platters were called chargers. Owing to the fact that the rims were decorated with a series of dashes or strokes in blue, which was one of the few pigments then available to the English potters, these plates are known to collectors as Blue Dash Chargers. They were produced at Liverpool, as well as in Staffordshire, toward the end of the Seventeenth Century and until about 1720. There is one charger dated 1668, bearing a portrait of Charles II. Another, with the portrait of the same king, depicts him escaping from the battle of Worcester disguised as a serving maid. The historic oak-apple tree in which he sought refuge is shown in the background.

Dishes with rather crude attempts at portraiture (usually inscribed with initials for identification) were also made at Bristol and Lambeth, as well as in Staffordshire, in imitation of the then popular Delft ware. At about the same period, Thomas Toft of Shelton and his brothers, James and Ralph, made a number of attempts at portrait platters, decorated in slip, and usually inscribed with their own names in large characters on the face of the dish.

John Dwight established his factory at Fulham about 1685. He was an artist, a sculptor of great talent, a gentleman, and an Oxford graduate. As he died in 1703, it is evident that the remarkable busts he modeled were produced in the late years of the Seventeenth Century. Even Enoch Wood and Wedgwood, half a century later, produced nothing to surpass in technique or artistry Dwight's bust of

Prince Rupert, which now rests in the British Museum. Dwight made many other noteworthy portrait pieces,—notably a bust of James II, and several figures of his little daughter, Lydia.

Of the Staffordshire potters, Astbury and Whieldon were among the first to produce figures. These were mostly fanciful, although many still exist portraying historical personages. There is a bust of the Duke of Cumberland by Wheildon in the Willett Collection, at Brighton.

It was the Wood family, however,—Ralph and Aaron, and their sons, Ralph and Enoch—of Burslem, who were the fathers of ceramic portraiture in England. They made many statuettes, mostly of mythological and romantic characters, and were the first of the English figure makers to mark their wares. Ralph Wood, the elder, who lived from 1715 to 1772, inscribed his pieces "R. Wood";—his son, who lived from 1748 to 1795, used the mark "Ra. Wood." Many such marked pieces exist in both public and private collections, but there are a greater number of unmarked pieces more or less justly ascribed to these prolific artists.

Among the pieces by the elder Ralph Wood, portraying individuals or fictional characters, are the Dutch Admiral Van Tromp, Lord Mayor Beckford, Britannia, St. George and the Dragon, and Hudibras. By the younger Ralph Wood, there are busts of Handel and Milton; figures of Sir Isaac Newton,

KING CHARLES II

Slip-ware dish picturing Charles II (1660-1685)
hiding in the Boscobel oak. Diameter, 18 inches.
Signed Thomas Toft. Staffordshire, c. 1670.

KING GEORGE I

Slip-ware dish decorated with an equestrian figure
and inscribed with the initials of George I (1714-
1727). Diameter, 13 inches. Staffordshire, c. 1720.

Metropolitan Museum

John Wilkes, Benjamin Franklin, Falstaff, Hercules, Neptune and Venus.

But Enoch, the youngest of the Woods, was the most talented of all, and ranks high among British sculptors. Born in 1759, under George II, he outlived George III, who had the longest reign of any English king; he lived through the reigns of George IV, of William IV, and saw the beginning of Queen Victoria's rule, dying at eighty-one years of age, in 1840. His life was equally divided between the Eighteenth and the Nineteenth Centuries; his days spanned the reigns of the French kings, Louis XV, Louis XVI, Louis XVIII, Charles X and Louis Philippe; of Frederick the Great of Prussia; Catherine the Great of Russia; the French Revolution; Napoleon, and the ten-year nightmare of the Napoleonic wars; the War of the American Revolution, and the War of 1812. He was a contemporary of John Wesley; of Nelson, Wellington, Howe and Rodney; of Pitt, Fox, Canning and Burke; of Voltaire, Lafayette, Washington and Franklin. What a span of life! He surely could not have accomplished this if, in his time, there had been daily papers, motor cars and telephones.

Enoch Wood was industrious, prolific and inventive. He created hundreds of models, many of which were shamelessly copied by other potters, as was unfortunately the custom of that period. He was progressive, being one of the first potters to make "old blue," and to market his wares in America. He was enthusiastically interested in his own art. He assembled a numerous and valuable collection of pottery dating as far back as the crude ceramic period of Charles II, and fully representative of the developments in his own time. This collection was dispersed a few years before his death; the greater part being divided among the museums of the three British capitals,—London, Edinburgh and Dublin. The remainder was purchased by the King of Saxony and is now preserved in Dresden.

But no doubt the most famous of all the English potters was Josiah Wedgwood, a contemporary of Enoch Wood, although thirty years his senior. He was even more inventive and more progressive than Wood. He was, however, a great potter rather than a fine artist. He was an administrator who knew how to attract to his service the most capable men, such as William Hackwood and John Flaxman, and to make the greatest use of their talents. His own best work was done in the technical and industrial branches of the industry. It was due to Wedgwood's foresight and energy that the Mersey Canal was put through, thus making it possible for the potteries to ship their wares to the far ends of the earth. Like Wood, he was scandalously imitated and plagiarized, but he nevertheless emerged as the foremost master of the craft.

Wedgwood produced portrait pieces both in figures and busts almost too numerous to mention. When he first developed his cream ware, he not only produced great quantities and varieties of dinner services, but he modeled figures of Milton, Shakespeare, Vandyke and of many mythological characters. Later he devised black basaltes, and used this material extensively for the making of busts, medallions and intaglios. He portrayed Bacon, Ben Jonson, Voltaire, Cato, Seneca and many others. Specimens of most of these are preserved in the Victoria and Albert Museum, London, as well as in the Wedgwood Museum at Etruria.

But his jasper ware was probably the most exquisite medium in which Wedgwood executed portraits. The jasper cameo placques alone form a portrait gallery of great beauty and importance. No complete collection of them exists, as many medallion portraits were made to the order of private individuals and members of the nobility, some of whom actually came to Etruria and sat for their portraits. Only a few copies of such private portraits were produced. The most complete collection of Wedgwood medallions is in the Liverpool Museum, and the finest private collection is owned by a London barrister. In the Wedgwood Memorial Institute, at Burslem, there is a fine array of these jasper pieces, and many of the original moulds and wax models are still preserved there.

It was during the last quarter of the Eighteenth Century that the practice of transfer printing, discovered or invented about 1750, was developed to such an extent as in some respects to revolutionize the potting industry. Until then the only known methods of decorating pottery were by slip, applied ornament, incision, or painting and enameling by hand. Transfer printing immediately made it possible to decorate any number of pieces of any shape with exactly the same design. A picture, or motif, is engraved on a copper plate; a print of this is taken on tissue paper which is applied to the ware, and the pigment rubbed in. The piece is then fired. By this method it is just as easy to transfer a design to a round teapot as to a flat plate.

When transfer printing first came into use, it was applied in black on the glaze; the object was then fired a second time, at a lower heat, with the result that the coloring matter was to a certain extent absorbed by the glaze, and gave somewhat the appearance of having been applied underglaze. Later, about 1780, actual underglaze printing was devised, and, as the art progressed, other colors than black were converted to decorative use. The favorite colors for jugs were black, mulberry, brown and red; cobalt blue, which did not alter in the firing, was the most popular pigment for tea sets, dishes, platters and plates,—so much so that a vast industry was developed in the making of blue plates alone. The willow pattern was probably the first of the famous blue plate designs, but, at the close of the War of 1812, when Britain first realized that a great market for its wares lay overseas, the Staffordshire potters, Enoch Wood among the first, began to make plates and dinner sets of old blue, decorated with American historic scenes.

The collection of these is an important phase of American ceramic interest, and several extensive and valuable collections of what has come to be called "Old Blue" have been assembled, and, unfortunately, some of them have been recently dispersed. I say "unfortunately," because after a collector had succeeded in gathering several hundred different specimens—which constituted almost a complete record of the products of the Staffordshire potteries in this most interesting field, and which would almost certainly never be brought together under one ownership again,— it seems deplorable that such a collection should have to go under the hammer. It should have been kept intact, and preserved in one of our great museums.

In November, 1925, the collection of Old Blue formed by the late George Kellogg of Amsterdam, N. Y., was sold at auction in New York. This collection had long been regarded as the finest of its kind in existence. For several of the pieces Mr. Kellogg had paid record prices—notably $1,225 for the "New York from Weehawk" platter, which at that time was the largest price ever paid for a piece of Old Blue. The collection included twelve specimens of the arms of the original thirteen states, New Hampshire alone being missing. This design is supposed to have been made, but no example of it has ever been found, either here or in England. It is said that Mr. Kellogg once refused an offer of $50,000 for this set of twelve armorial pieces. This is regrettable, if true, for when the collection was eventually dispersed in New York, the total realized for the four hundred or more pieces was $30,490,—which would seem to indicate that the story of the $50,000 offer for twelve pieces is apocryphal, or that the maker of that offer failed at the time of the sale to take advantage of a wonderful opportunity.

Comparatively few portraits were made on plates, and these were usually of subordinate importance, inserted in medallions as a part of the decoration, the principal design on the ware being scenic. There are Rochester Aqueduct, the Park Theatre, Niagara and other plates by Stevenson & Williams with four medallion portraits of Washington, Lafayette, Jefferson and Clinton, and several other designs with portraits of Washington and Lafayette, or Washington and Clinton, or Jefferson and Lafayette.

Liverpool, Leeds, Worcester and Sunderland were the leaders in the new art of transfer printing, and many exquisite portrait mugs and jugs were produced by those potteries. Excellent examples of these are preserved in the Liverpool Museum, as well as in the Royal Porcelain Works Museum at Worcester. There, notably, are a mug with a transfer print portrait of George II, and a vase with a portrait of George III. In Sunderland, a great industry was developed in the manufacture of Sunderland jugs

H. H. Costain

KING GEORGE IV AND QUEEN CAROLINE JUGS

(See pages 69 and 111)

and mugs, most of them bearing prints of the Iron Bridge across the River Wear.

When, in the early years of the Nineteenth Century, the art of transfer printing on pottery had come into general use, the English potters began rather extensively to commemorate historical events and individuals on jugs, drinking mugs, and frequently on trays or placques. Milk jugs and beer jugs being of daily use in the homes and taverns of England, these no doubt seemed to the potters the obvious vehicles for the exploitation of heroes and the dissemination of political propaganda. They were in a sense the predecessors of our illustrated comic and satirical periodicals.

Especially during those years when Napoleon was ravaging Europe and threatening to invade England, were the vituperation and ridicule of English patriots expressed in virulent cartoons on jugs. In the Willett Collection there are about fifty examples of these; and, even today, in the antique shops, one not infrequently comes upon desirable pieces in fairly good condition. Indeed, I picked up two in Chelsea, one of which was quite perfect, and the other but slightly time-cracked and stained inside from use.

After Napoleon had been disposed of, the cartoonists turned their satire against their own Kings, George IV and William IV, particularly in connection with the divorcing of Queen Caroline in 1820, and the passing of the Reform Laws in 1832. The resentment of the English people against George IV for his ruffianly treatment of Queen Caroline was freely and bitterly expressed. Caroline jugs were produced in great variety, ranging from vessels of the commonest clay imprinted with derisive verses, to exquisite pieces decorated with cameo portraits and relief ornamentation, of high artistic merit. There is also a considerable variety of Reform jugs, mostly printed in mulberry tones; and many different types and shapes bearing portraits of William IV and Queen Adelaide, Lord John Russell, Lord Brougham and other statesmen of that period.

CHAPTER VI

IN the early years of Queen Victoria's reign, as roads were bettered and transportation facilities (particularly for so frail a product as chinaware) became improved, a large trade was developed in what the potteries designated as "cottage ornaments,"—earthenware figures of national and legendary heroes, romantic characters of fiction, bucolic types, and animals in great variety. The early attempts of the Staffordshire modelers,—excepting, of course, those of such genuine artists as Enoch Wood, Josiah Wedgwood, Ralph Salt and one or two others,—were rather crude, but, with the growing demand for these decorative products, their quality improved; and although, in the opinion of many, these cottage ornaments may never rank as works of ceramic art, they nevertheless possess a charm, a virility and a personality which gained for them then, and still holds for them now, a place in the affection of all who have a fondness for vigor, simplicity and sincerity.

These statuettes and figures were called cottage ornaments because, usually sold at the fairs, they were distributed throughout the rural communities, and their popularity was such that in the mid-Victorian era, there was scarcely a cottage chimney

71

piece in all of England ungraced by a Sailor and his Lass, Robin Hood and Friar Tuck, Nelson and Wellington, or other brightly colored earthenware groups, figures or animals. These ornaments, especially as to figures, were usually made in pairs, that they might stand stiffly at either end of the mantelshelf, or upon either corner of the highboy. Groups such as the "Babes in the Wood" or the "Death of Nelson" being more elaborate attempts at plastic art, were seldom, if ever, made in pairs, doubtless being intended as central ornaments in the prim and symmetric decorative scheme of the period.

Wellington, Nelson and John Wesley were the favorite heroes of the early Nineteenth Century Staffordshire potters. Wellington achieved so great an eminence as warrior and statesman, and enjoyed so long a life, that it would be now quite impossible to enumerate or record the hundreds of different pieces of pottery that were produced in his honor and commemoration. He was born in 1769 and died in 1852.

The unbroken splendors of his military career, his honorable and conscientious labors as a parliamentary statesman place Wellington among the great Englishmen of history. To commemorate his defeat of the French at Vittoria, under King Joseph, Napoleon's elder brother, some exquisite pieces in the form of jugs and mugs were produced, probably by Ridgways, about 1810. These are of a drab stoneware with applied figure decorations in low relief, and bands of rich blue enamel circling the rim of the mug and the rim and shoulder of the jug. The handle of the latter is modeled at the upper part as the head of a lion decorated in the natural colors. The relief figure decorations show Wellington on horseback being acclaimed by his officers, one of whom is presenting him with a field marshal's baton, the other waving a scarf inscribed "Vittoria." Other figures on the jug are two British soldiers dragging a captured cannon and eagles toward an orange tree under which stands a large box inscribed "Plunder," bulging with church ornaments and gold and silver plate, —a quaint sidelight on the predatory practices of warfare in those days. A mug of this design and coloring, the only one I have seen with the exception of my own jug, may be noticed in the Victoria and Albert Museum, South Kensington, No. 3,635.

Countless face-jugs of Wellington, of the toby-jug type, were produced, as we have previously noted, in Staffordshire, at Lambeth and at Rackingham; but after Wellington, the conqueror, became Wellington, the statesman, the potters began to produce figures of him in the formal citizen's dress of the late William IV and early Victorian periods. Many of these are rather fancifully colored, for it seems doubtful that Wellington ever attired himself in pink or lavender trousers; but the best models are usually in white and gold.

Figures of Nelson are not so numerous as jugs, which were made in every fashion,—figure-jugs, face-jugs, and countless jugs with transfer printed portraits, emblems, maps and inscriptions. A beautiful black basaltes tea set was produced by Wedgwood shortly after Nelson's death. The sides of the teapot, cream jug and sugar basin are decorated with raised and exquisitely modeled designs. On one side Britannia is shown standing at Nelson's tomb, where an angel is inscribing the hero's name. On the other, on either side of a trophy of arms and flags, are a pyramid and a castle, the former commemorative of the Battle of the Nile, the latter of the Battle of Copenhagen. The workmanship of these diminutive bas-reliefs is so exquisite that it will bear careful examination through a magnifying glass.

Several groups were made picturing Nelson's death at Trafalgar. One of these is particularly effective and was probably done in Burslem, as late as 1830 or 1840, which was the period when the potters were becoming actively interested in modeling figures and groups for a rapidly expanding market. The piece is seven inches high, richly colored and glazed, and inscribed in gold script "Death of Nelson." The Admiral is represented in a recumbent posture, just as he fell on the deck of the "Victory," after being shot by a French rifleman from the rigging of the "Redoubtable." A figure on the left, supporting Nelson and offering him a glass of water, is Dr. Scott, the chaplain of the "Victory." The figure on the right, kneeling beside Nelson and holding his hand, is Mr. Beatty, the flagship's surgeon. In Eng-

H. H. Costain

ADMIRAL, LORD NELSON

The Admiral is represented as he fell on the deck of the "Victory" at the battle of Trafalgar. The group is historically accurate, the figure on the left holding a glass being Dr. Scott, the chaplain of the "Victory," and that on the right, kneeling, the ship's surgeon, Mr. Beatty. Height, 7 inches. Staffordshire, c. 1850. (See page 74.)

land a surgeon is always addressed as "Mr.," never as "Dr."

In this group there is only a vague attempt at portraiture, Nelson being pictured with two perfectly good wide-open eyes; but it is quite accurate in its representation of the actual occurrence. Nelson's death was indirectly due to his proud persistence in wearing his full admiral's uniform and decorations not only daily but in battle. On the day of Trafalgar he appeared as usual with his "four stars" showing brilliantly on the breast of his frock coat,—ornaments rendering him so conspicuous to the enemy, in those days of fighting at close quarters, that his officers were more than usually concerned. It was known to them that there were riflemen aboard the French ships. Dr. Scott, the chaplain, was urged by the other officers to entreat Nelson to change his dress or cover the stars. But he hesitated to do so, knowing that such a request would highly displease him. To previous similar suggestions Nelson had replied sternly: "In honor I gained them, in honor I will die with them." And so it came to pass.

The French ship "Redoubtable" was the nearest to the "Victory," shortly after noon, the battle having begun early in the morning. Twice Nelson had given orders to cease firing upon her, supposing that she had struck, because her guns were silent and her flag had been shot away. From this ship, which he had twice spared, he received his death. A sharpshooter in the "Redoubtable's" mizzen top, crouch-

75

ing not more than fifteen yards from where Nelson
stood on the quarter deck of the "Victory," sent a
bullet which hit Nelson in the epaulette on his left
shoulder, passing downward to the spine. The Admiral fell upon his face. Captain Hardy turned to
see Dr. Scott and Mr. Beatty raising him up. Nelson
exclaimed: "They have done for me, Hardy; my
backbone is shot through!" Thus does Southey
describe that historic scene.

He tells, too, that in 1825, there was published
a book purporting to have been written by Robert
Guillemart, a French sergeant of fusiliers, who declared it was a shot from his rifle which brought
down the English Admiral. He stated: "On the poop
of the English vessel was an officer covered with
orders, and with only one arm. From what I had
heard of Nelson, I had no doubt that it was he. . . .
As I had received no orders to go down, and saw
myself forgotten in the tops, I thought it my duty
to fire on the poop of the English vessel, which I
saw quite exposed and close to me. I could even have
taken aim at the men I saw, but I fired at hazard
among the groups I saw of sailors and officers. All
at once I saw great confusion on board the 'Victory';
the men crowded round the officer whom I had taken
for Nelson. He had just fallen, and was carried
below, covered with a cloak. The agitation shown
at this moment left me no doubt that I had judged
rightly, and that it really was the English admiral.
. . . From the moment he received his wound, and

the position of the wound itself, I could not doubt for a moment that I was the author; and I have ever since been fully convinced of it. But though the shot that had brought down this admiral had rendered a service to my country, I was far from considering it as an action of which I had a right to boast. Besides, in the general confusion, everyone could claim the honour."

But, of the three British national characters,—Wellington, Nelson and Wesley,—who so greatly inspired the potters, the Rev. John Wesley seems to have appealed most strongly to their imaginations. Wellington and Nelson were national heroes, but Wesley seems to have become a sort of personal hero to the potters. It would perhaps be no exaggeration to state that every Staffordshireman, having any skill as a modeler, made a bust or a figure, of one kind or another, of the great Methodist. Those potters who were not modelers transfer-printed his countenance on teapots, plates, mugs, jugs and placques. There is one private collection of Wesleyana, in England, containing over four hundred portraits, including busts, Wedgwood medallions and transfer-printed pieces, together with a superb bust after Roubillac.

Wesley made two visits to the Staffordshire potteries, and created a great impression by his preaching. On the occasion of his second visit, in 1781, he stayed at the house of Enoch Wood where the latter, who was then only twenty two, modeled the large portrait bust which, with that of Whitefield, done later, is considered among the best of Wood's achievements. Wood also modeled smaller busts which were imitated and pirated by countless other potters. Wedgwood produced a black basaltes bust of Wesley, and Felix Pratt modeled a head which is noteworthy for its benign and idealistic expression. The lesser potters of Longton Hall and Burslem, in fact of the entire countryside, produced various statuettes of Wesley in his canonical robes, and a variety of cottage pieces, such as watch-stands and spill-vases, picturing Wesley preaching from the pulpit. These pulpit pieces are frequently decorated with angels and cherubs floating in wooly clouds above the preacher's head. Many of them are of ornate and almost clumsy workmanship, but ingenuously expressive of genuine sincerity.

The important Welsey portraits mentioned above were produced at the period when the art of plastic potting in Staffordshire had reached its highest degree of artistic merit. It was during the last quarter of the Eighteenth Century that the great potters of Staffordshire performed their best work, and no English potters since their time have surpassed these accomplishments. This was the period of Josiah Wedgwood, Flaxman, Ralph and Enoch Wood, Adams, Turner, Spode, Neale, to mention but a few.

The decadence began toward the end of the first quarter of the Nineteenth Century. Quantity then began to displace quality, especially in the making

H. H. Costain

THE REV. JOHN WESLEY

(See page 77)

of cottage figures and statuettes. Soon after the accession of Victoria, almost every little pottery found it profitable to produce portrait pieces of popular or eminent characters, and thus a vast number of inferior pieces, original and copied, came into being.

Statuettes of Queen Victoria and her consort, Prince Albert, were produced in endless variety. Victoria is almost always represented by the Staffordshire potters as wearing a crown of more or less simple design, a bodice cut low at the neck and shoulders,—or at least as low as was Victorianly proper, —and a long full skirt consisting of several circular flounces, the edges of which are almost invariably decorated with small pink roses.

A collection of statuettes of Victoria would depict her only from her young maidenhood (when she became Queen at the age of eighteen, in 1837), until a period not later than 1855. I know of no pottery statuette portraying her in her later years, except the beautiful Doulton salt-glazed stoneware figure, representing the Queen in full regalia, seated on the throne, modeled by John Broad for the Diamond Jubilee in 1897.

There are several pseudo-portrait groups, produced at the time of the Crimean War, 1853-55; but in all these Victoria is represented as still a very young woman. Indeed she had not yet become widowed and portly. These groups were made at a time when there was great enthusiasm in England for the French, and even for the Turks. The three nations were united in war against Russia. Most of these pieces represent Victoria and Napoleon III standing with clasped hands; one ingenuous group shows Victoria standing between Napoleon and the Sultan Abdul Medjid, holding each fondly by the hand, the rulers of France and Turkey looking fairly self-conscious. This group is labeled "Turkey, England, France."

In the Willett Collection, which contains twenty-eight Victorian pieces, there is no statuette of Victoria of a later date than 1841; this is a Staffordshire group of the Queen with a child, probably intended to represent the Princess Royal. In point of chronology, the next portrait of Victoria, in the Willett Collection, is a printed mug made at the time of the Golden Jubilee in 1887; and the only modeled portrait after the 1841 group is a bust made for the Diamond Jubilee of 1897, portraying her as she appeared at that time.

Either Victoria was sensitive at being portrayed at an age beyond young womanhood, or the potters preferred to continue perpetuating their Queen in her more youthful aspect. Nevertheless, it is perhaps a curious coincidence that although, in her long reign, the frame designs of England's postage stamps were altered many times, yet the same profile portrait of the young Victoria which graced the first postal issue of 1840, was retained on every issue of English postage stamps until her death. Some of the Colonies, notably Canada and Newfoundland, diverged from this adherence.

Albert Edward, Prince of Wales, afterward Edward VII, was potted from his earliest youth. There is a statuette of Victoria holding in her arms a baby in long clothes,—which is Albert Edward. There is a mounted figure labeled "Prince of Wales" picturing Albert Edward at about the age of twenty. There are various large pieces, gaily colored, some labeled and some unmarked, showing the Prince in manhood with full beard and attired in military uniform. There are companion pieces, too, portraying "The Prince of Wales" and the "Princess of Wales," later Queen Alexandra; and there are equestrian pairs, labeled "Prince" and "Princess," which are usually in white and gold.

In the early part of the Nineteenth Century, as we have noted, and before Victoria's time, the Staffordshire potters developed an important trade with the United States, and catered to this by the manufacture of a great variety of pictorial designs in blue tableware decorated with American views. But this market eventually became oversupplied, or some other economic factor interfered, with the result that by the middle of the century what had once been a great export business had dwindled practically to nothing.

Nevertheless the potters still kept America in mind, and in that period when the making of statuettes and figures had become one of the most popular and profitable developments of the industry, figures of American subjects began to be modeled and produced.

Mrs. Harriet Beecher Stowe's *Uncle Tom's Cabin* was first published in book form in 1852, and its sensational success spread immediately to England. It seems strange that the English, who in so many ways expressed their scorn for a government that permitted slavery, should have been, in the subsequent American controversy, actively antagonistic to the side which was struggling for the emancipation of the negroes. But I suppose trade in cotton is one thing, and ideals are another.

At any rate, soon after *Uncle Tom's Cabin* became familiar to British readers, the Staffordshire potters began to produce figures of Uncle Tom and statuette groups of Uncle Tom and Little Eva. There are several variations of these. There are three different ones in the Willett Collection, and I have seen others. The one most frequently to be found represents Uncle Tom sitting on a rock with his arm about Little Eva, who stands on his knee with her left hand resting on the old negro's shoulder. The piece is inscribed: "Eva gaily laughing was hanging a wreath of roses around Tom's neck,"—a proceeding which, in the statuette, gives Uncle Tom a decidedly Hawaiian appearance.

Ridgways produced a series of jugs in the usual three sizes elaborately decorated in low relief with

Omer Pacha

Gen. Pélissier

Napoleon III and Victoria

King and Queen of Sardinia

Abdul Medjid, Victoria, Napoleon III

CRIMEAN WAR PIECES
(See pages 79 and 216)

A. C. *Shaw*

scenes from Mrs. Stowe's book. The jugs are of a uniform grayish green colored stoneware, and the top of the handle is modeled as the head and shoulders of Uncle Tom with his hands clasped in prayer. On one side of the jug is a representation of a slave auction. The auctioneer, with gavel in hand, stands in a rostrum on the front of which is the inscription: "By Auction This Day, a Prime Lot of Healthy NEGROES." At the right is a group of three planters, with long cigars sticking out of their mouths, one of whom has his hand raised in bidding. On the left of the auctioneer a negro slave is shown on the auction block; his daughter stands near by covering her face in despair, while his wife, holding a baby on her lap, sits weeping on a bench in the foreground.

On the other side of the jug is a scene representing Eliza escaping across the ice with her child in her arms, pursued by Haley, wildly brandishing a whip. Eliza is quite elaborately costumed, and wears a poke bonnet with a gay bow upon it. Harry is also completely attired in his best Sunday clothes, and clings sturdily to Eliza's neck as he looks back at the pursuing trader. The cakes of ice are ingenuously modeled, but nevertheless Eliza seems to find a safe foothold upon them. (See facing page 178.)

The jug is marked on the base with the characteristic Ridgway raised imprint:

PUBLISHED BY
RIDGWAY & ABINGDON
JANUARY 1, 1853

Staffordshire produced several portrait busts of Mrs. Stowe, and, when the Civil War came, the potters portrayed Lincoln. But these pieces are rare, and I have seen but one Staffordshire Lincoln, an equestrian figure of considerable merit. This was probably produced between 1861 and 1865.

Lincoln is shown mounted on a typical prancing Staffordshire horse. This same animal, in almost the identical pose, appears in other statuettes, bearing the Duke of Cambridge, or the Prince of Wales, or other military heroes. Lincoln's horse is in white, with the conventional exception of nose and hoofs, but his mane, bridle and tail are penciled in silver instead of in gold, as is the case with most equine models of that period. The saddle is red.

The portraiture of Lincoln is good, although his hair and beard are rather more reddish than in nature, and his complexion is perhaps a trifle too florid. He sits his horse well. He wears a frock coat and a low-cut four-buttoned waistcoat. About his shoulders hangs a long red cloak with a heavy fur collar. His right hand rests on the horse's head and the tasseled reins dangle from his fingers. His left hand rests on the saddle by his side, holding his hat,––but the limitations of potting made it necessary to reduce the stature of this headgear to such a degree that it resembles a closed opera hat, rather than the traditional stovepipe so characteristic of the president. To make up for this deficiency the potter has added gay little silver tassels to the brim.

H. H. Costain

ABRAHAM LINCOLN

Earthenware statuette, 15 inches high. In general effect the piece is of white and silver, although the saddle and cloak are bright red, and the face and hands are in the natural colors. The inscription is in Egyptian lettering. Staffordshire, c. 1865. (See page 84.)

On the base of the statuette appears the name "A. LINCOLN," in raised block letters penciled in silver. These block letters date the piece fairly accurately, as this style of inscription was not generally adopted in Staffordshire until about 1860, and came into general use in the mid-Victorian period,—that is, between 1860 and 1880. It had been used at Lambeth at an earlier date, as may be noted from the inscriptions on the bases of the Albert and Victoria flasks shown facing page 132.

In later years, with the development and refinement of transfer printing, jugs with portraits of American characters were made by various potters. American merchants also placed orders in England for the making of certain portrait pieces, principally jugs. In 1880 Richard Briggs, of Boston, designed and commissioned the Wedgwood pottery to make a jug bearing a portrait of Longfellow. The first one to reach America was presented to the poet, who was a friend of Mr. Briggs, and Mr. Longfellow wrote a letter of acknowledgment. Five thousand of these jugs were made and sold, even at that period, at five dollars each. Occasionally today one of them turns up in an auction sale, but not very frequently. What has become of those five thousand jugs?

Mr. Briggs retained one copy of the Longfellow jug and upon his death, several years ago, this was presented by his son, together with the Longfellow letter, to Mr. Henry Ford with the understanding that these should be preserved and exhibited at the Wayside Inn, Sudbury, Mass.

In 1890 Mr. Briggs ordered from Wedgwood a Tennyson jug, of which only one thousand copies were made, and also a jasper ware portrait medallion of Oliver Wendell Holmes, of which there was produced but a very limited edition.

CHAPTER VII

T was not only the Staffordshire potters who made portrait pieces. A very numerous and interesting group of these was produced in salt-glazed stoneware at Lambeth, Fulham and in Derbyshire, beginning as early as the middle of the Eighteenth Century and continuing at Lambeth even until our own time. Most of these portrait pieces are in the form of flasks, but there are also several toby-jugs and face-jugs. The flasks were originally made for the use of the inns in dispensing spirits in small quantities. The weight of these must have been quite an impediment to trade. In the beginning they were void of any decoration, but frequently had the name of the inn or innkeeper, or both, impressed upon them. In the early 1800's ornament began to be applied, first in simple wreaths or bunches of grapes, and later with figures or groups in low relief. The next development was to mould the top of the flask to represent the head and shoulders of a man. This form achieved great popularity as a vehicle for political satire, under William IV, when the Reform Laws were the absorbing political issue of the day.

There are Lambeth flasks, by Stephen Green and Doulton & Watts, representing King William IV, Lord Brougham, Lord John Russell, Earl Grey, and the Irish patriot, Daniel O'Connell. Similar pieces were made in Derbyshire. The latter usually bear an impressed mark on the bottom "Belper and Denby, Bourne's Potteries, Derbyshire." In the early years of the Nineteenth Century, Doulton & Watts produced portrait-jugs of Nelson and Napoleon, of a high quality of portraiture.

Doulton & Company, Lambeth, carried on the tradition of portraying political characters in the form of stoneware spirit flasks, and as late as 1912 produced a series of six, from models by L. Harradine, portraying the leading political figures of the day:—Mr. Herbert Asquith, the then Prime Minister; Mr. David Lloyd George, then Chancellor of the Exchequer and later War Premier of the Coalition Cabinet; Mr. Arthur James Balfour, who had been Prime Minister from 1902 to 1905; Viscount Haldane, the Lord High Chancellor; Mr. Austen Chamberlain, M.P., and Mr. John Burns, the noted British Labor Leader.

The flasks follow the conventional design and coloring of those produced in the time of William IV, except that they bear no inscriptions. The lower portion of each piece is of a deep buff color; the upper part, to the waist, of a darker, browner shade, each piece before firing having been dipped. In 1923, a new edition of these flasks, cast in the original moulds, was produced. These later ones, however, owing to a difference in the clay mixture and the dipping solution, are of a much lighter coloring.

LORD BROUGHAM.   KING WILLIAM IV.   LORD BROUGHAM.

DANIEL O'CONNELL.   DANIEL O'CONNELL.   LORD GREY.

Saltglazed stoneware spirit flasks, made during the turbulent political period of the
reign of William IV (1830-1837) when the Reform Laws and Catholic Emancipation
were under discussion in Parliament. Doulton and Watts, Lambeth 1832. (See page 87.)

From the Doulton Collection

Flasks were similarly made at Rockingham in glazed brownware, among others Princess Charlotte, Queen Victoria, and Dr. Johnson. All these stoneware pieces display a much higher quality and greater accuracy of portraiture than are to be found in the early Victorian Staffordshire figures.

The most popular of the Victorian stoneware flasks, if one may judge from the fact that they are still not infrequently to be found in the London antique shops, is the one modeled in relief with portraits of Mr. and Mrs. Caudle, from the drawing by Charles Keene, made to illustrate one of Douglas Jerrold's "Mrs. Caudle's Curtain Lectures," published by *Punch* in 1846. The flask is of approximately that date, although many later editions of it have been produced. The latter are usually unmarked; the original pieces bear the Doulton imprint.

It was not alone on flasks, jugs and statuettes that the potters indulged in portraiture. They modeled faces on such odd and diversified articles as doorknobs, cane handles, paper weights, inkstands, birdseed holders and furniture rests, which have already been referred to on page 34. The head of Princess Charlotte appears on rests made in brown Rockingham ware. She is readily recognized by her curls. Occasionally these rests were decorated in full color; but as a rule they are of a brown monotone to harmonize with the wood of the furniture.

The birdseed holders are extremely amusing and

very decorative, but quite rare. No doubt the parlor maids of the Georgian era saw to that.

The inkstands were usually round and flat, being indeed masks only. The open mouth served as the receptacle for the writing fluid and a hole in the forehead was used as a rest for the quill pen. I have one portraying Dr. Johnson. It is of brown, richly glazed earthenware, bearing on the back the impressed mark of Joseph Thompson, Brampton. Most of these ink pots were caricatures, the best known of which are those of John Ridgway and his wife, which are upright heads about three and a half inches high. Ridgway is the potter whose products are probably the best known and the most collected in America. It was he who produced the greatest variety of blue and white china, with views of American scenery. It is said that some unfriendly rival modeled these ink pots, and so good were the lampoons that the members of the Ridgway family bought up every specimen they could lay their hands on. They are colored in enamel and are said to be excellent, if unkind, portraits. None of the Staffordshire museums possess examples, with the exception of Hanley which has one of the John Ridgway inkstands. Inferior copies were produced later in stoneware, specimens of which are occasionally to be met with. They lack, however, the vitality and personality of the original models.

The Staffordshire figures of the mid-Victorian period, except of contemporary royal personages and of celebrities such as Nelson or Wellington, seldom offer more than a remote claim of actual resemblance to the originals; but the identity of these is usually indicated by an inscription, where not already clearly apparent by the action represented. There is a white and gold group of two bearded cavaliers, in rolling boots and feathered hats, labeled "King Charles and Cromwell." Here is the only occasion on which I have seen Cromwell portrayed with a beard; but, after all, what is a beard more or less to a Staffordshire potter who needed a bit of color to add character to his product? And, even if these particular figures bear no real resemblance to the King and the Commoner, even if they are not exact portraits, (and that of the King is really not bad), the group is ingenuously intended to represent these worthies and is so labeled that there may be no mistake about it.

Occasionally one comes upon portrait pieces with incorrect inscriptions,—so placed either by carelessness or, in some cases, deliberately. The Franklin and Washington figures by Wood are the most conspicuous examples of such inadvertence, Washington being labeled Franklin, and Franklin being labeled Washington. There are not many genuine examples of these errors, as the careless potter was apparently stopped before he had gotten very far along in his nefarious procedure. But there are a number of forgeries of these mislabeled figures.

There is one Staffordshire statuette which, some skeptical collectors believe, has for a long time mas-

queraded as a figure of Benjamin Franklin. In Mr.
Blacker's *A. B. C. of Old English Pottery,* there is
a pen and ink drawing of this piece. In the type-
caption, printed underneath, the figure is entitled
"Benjamin Franklin," although no lettering appears
on the square pedestal, whose only decoration is an
oval medallion. Mr. Blacker attributes the piece to
Ralph Wood, Jr., and he is doubtless correct, for the
square pedestal with a rosette in relief is typical of
the younger Wood. He used this design on several
authenticated pieces. An example of this same statuette is included in the Willett Collection (No. 451)
and is illustrated in the catalogue and listed as
"Benjamin Franklin, Burslem 1770."

In the Museum of Practical Geology, London
(No. G 374, before many of the collections were
moved to another museum), was an example of this
same statuette, described as "Dr. Franklin, height
13 ¼ inches, mounted on square marbled pedestal
with oval medallions in relief."

Another specimen is included in the Huntington
Collection at the Metropolitan Museum, New York,
but here, in addition to the rosette, the pedestal bears
the inscription "Dr. Franklin." Some keen observer
has raised the question as to whether this statuette
was originally intended as a portrait of Benjamin
Franklin, contending that it was actually designed
to represent William Pitt, Earl of Chatham. Pitt
(1708-1778) was two years younger than Franklin
(1706-1790). As the Ralph Wood figure was ap-

ARTHUR JAMES BALFOUR.   VISCOUNT HALDANE.   AUSTEN CHAMBERLAIN.

JOHN BURNS.   DAVID LLOYD GEORGE.   HERBERT ASQUITH.

Saltglazed stoneware spirit flasks, portraying the leading political figures of England just before the war. Height, 7½ inches. Doulton Lambeth, 1912. (See page 88.)

parently made in 1770, it would portray Pitt as he quite probably looked then, at the age of 62.

The arguments offered in favor of the Pitt portraiture are plausible. The statuettes in the Willett Collection and in the Museum of Practical Geology are original examples of Ralph Wood's modeling and bear no identifying inscriptions. Their pedestals have only the rosette decoration. The one in the Huntington Collection has the rosette and is additionally inscribed "Dr. Franklin." These words seem to appear only on pieces produced some fifteen or more years after the original model was issued. Forgeries of this figure have subsequently been made with the rosette eliminated, and merely the words "Dr. Franklin" inscribed upon the pedestal. The inferior quality of the decoration of the later pieces is clearly apparent when compared with the workmanship on a genuine specimen.

William Pitt, Earl of Chatham, as Secretary of State (1756-63) had earned high reputation by his successful direction of government policy during the Seven Years' War. But, ten years later, he lost much of this popularity, owing to his staunch partisanship for, and defence of, the American colonists in their struggle for independence.

It was, perhaps, after the Seven Years' War, and before the American Revolution, that Ralph Wood may have selected Pitt as a fit subject to perpetuate in clay. This theory coincides with the date, 1770, ascribed to the statuette by Mr Willett.

Franklin was sent to England in 1764 to contest the pretentions of Parliament to tax the American Colonies without representation. He returned to America in 1775, meantime having achieved considerable personal popularity during his residence in London. In 1776 he was sent to Paris where he remained as American Minister until 1785. In France his popularity was greater even than it had been in England. Portraits of him in almost every medium were numerously made in both countries.

Ralph Wood's figure, made in 1770, if intended as a statuette of Pitt, was perhaps not a success commercially, and its production may very well have been discontinued until it occurred to the potter, at Pitt's death in 1778, that by labeling the piece with Franklin's name,—the resemblance being sufficient to carry off the deception,—a certain commercial profit might be reaped.

Mrs. Alice Morse Earle, in *China Collecting in America* (published 1892) refers extensively to this piece, which she saw in the Museum of Practical Geology, and observes: "Dr. Franklin wears in this case white breeches, blue waistcoat, scarlet coat, a blue ribbon with an order, and a long ermine cloak. The statuette . . . at first glance is quite impressive. The Doctor, comparatively devoid of pendulous chin, stands erect and beautiful, with his head thrown back with a most imperious and even imperial air, to which the ermine cloak gives added weight and zest."

It is apparent that, without realizing why, Mrs. Earle was dubious about this statuette. She noticed the absence of Franklin's "pendulous chin"; she noted the "scarlet coat" and the "long ermine cloak." But Mrs. Earle was in error with respect to what she calls a "blue ribbon with an order." This is a monocle. Franklin never wore a monocle. The Earl of Chatham probably did. Neither would Franklin have worn a scarlet coat or a cloak trimmed with ermine, the royal fur. Indeed, there is no statuette that I know of showing Franklin wearing a draped cloak of any kind. On the other hand there are two beautiful Chelsea statuettes of Pitt, in the Metropolitan Museum, one in glazed white porcelain, the other with highly colored decoration, and both figures are shown draped in long cloaks. This cloak, as shown also in the Brompton portrait, was characteristic of Pitt's formal and ceremonial apparel; and, as a British peer, it was Pitt's prerogative to wear the scarlet and ermine. The attitude of the Ralph Wood figure is that of the forceful orator "with a most imperious and even imperial air." Such was Pitt. Poor Richard never was imperious, much less imperial. These are some of the outward indications that the figure may not be that of Franklin.

On the other hand, those conservatives who prefer to believe that the statuette was actually intended by Wood as a portrait of Franklin point out that the Earl of Chatham invariably wore a wig, whereas Franklin wore natural long hair, as modeled on the statuette. The skeptics retort that it would have been quite easy for Wood to remodel the hair when he transformed Pitt into Franklin,—if such was the case. But there is no record of any similar figure showing a wigged head! Here, therefore, is an interesting field for investigation by the collector of portrait statuettes.

Another instance of the deliberate mislabeling of a portrait at the hands of the potter himself appears on a placque made at Prestonpans, in Scotland, in 1822, portraying George IV, whose bloated countenance and heavy curls are recognizable at once by anyone familiar with Hanoverian portraiture. This King was exceedingly unpopular with the English people, particularly at the period immediately following the death of Queen Caroline. It seems to have occurred to George that visits to Ireland and Scotland might develop for him some slight popularity which was beyond his attainment in a country where he was better known. No English king had set foot in Scotland since Charles II in 1650. George IV visited Edinburgh in August 1822. Sir Walter Scott took a leading part in organizing the reception.

The excellently modeled and brightly colored placque, pictured facing page 104, was made as soon as the King's proposed visit was announced, and no doubt a considerable quantity of them was shipped for display and sale in the souvenir shops of Edinburgh. They were loyally inscribed in lettering impressed upon a broad ribbon, stretching across the lower portion of the royal bust: "Welcome George IV."

Now, the King's Scottish subjects may have been vociferous in their public acclaim of the sovereign, but they were apparently not very lavish in their expenditure for pottery portraits of his Majesty. The demand for the placque was negligible. Thus the potters found themselves with a lot of those placques on their hands, and, as it did not look as if there would be any further occasion to welcome George anywhere, the placques gathered dust in the warehouses for several years.

The King died in 1830, and was succeeded by his brother, William IV, third son of George III. William bore no facial resemblance to George, but this was not much of a factor with Scottish potters, when it came to unloading an accumulation of portrait placques. They proceeded to daub out the "Welcome George IV" with enamel paint, and ingenuously wrote underneath, in clumsy script "William the IVth Britiania." (The potters never were very good spellers.) This black inscription, having been applied overglaze, is easily detectable to the touch.

As to the figures and groups which bear no inscription, but where the identity of the character or characters is readily apparent from the action depicted, take for example the royal personage seated in a tent, signing an important looking document, with plumed pages at either side watching respectfully. This can be no other than "King John signing

Magna Charta.'' And when you come across a figure of an oriental young woman resting a jar upon what appears to be a stone wall, you know that you have ''Rebeka at the Well.'' If you are so fortunate as to find a group showing a bearded patriarch with two or three black birds placed where their wings may be easily broken by careless handling, you at once recognize ''Elijah and the Ravens.'' But, if any of the ravens' wings are missing, steel your heart against buying the damaged piece. Some day you will perhaps find another with all the ravens in perfect health.

There is yet a third classification among the portrait figures—not only of Staffordshire, but of all pottery,—which is sorely distressing to the collector whose familiarity with historical physiognomies cannot be all-embracing. They are those uninscribed pieces that may be jugs, or busts or statuettes and which, in their modeling and in their details of costume, give every indication of having been designed to portray some particular personage. The potted traits bear unequivocal conviction that here indeed is a true likeness.

The collector is now faced with a problem. A new element enters into the excitement of the chase. The portrait hunter has found a portrait,—but he must dispel the mystery that lies hidden in that mute glazed countenance; he must solve the enigma the very answer to which, so to speak, is staring him in the face.

BENJAMIN FRANKLIN OR
WILLIAM PITT?

The identity of this figure by Ralph Wood has been questioned. Several variants are known. (See pages 91-96.) The figure on the left is in the Huntington Collection, the other one is an early Nineteenth Century reproduction.

BENJAMIN FRANKLIN

Examples of the mislabelling of Franklin statuettes, both of these being inscribed "George Washington." Height, 15 inches. Staffordshire, c. 1800. (See page 91.)
Metropolitan Museum, New York

Sometimes the solution of the puzzle is not so very difficult, particularly with characters in naval or military uniform. Indeed, with English pottery, a little patience, research and observation will usually result in definite identification, for the English potters made few portraits of minor celebrities. But when it comes to continental pieces, of which there appears to be an infinite variety, the problem is frequently baffling. Yet we should not feel unduly disturbed at any lack of general acquaintance with the facial traits of French, German or Italian worthies whose deeds or personalities may have been perpetuated by the potters of Sèvres, Meissen or Capo di Monte. The continental potters made a far greater variety of portrait statuettes than the English, and modeled many who might now be designated merely as local celebrities, such as Eighteenth Century nobles of the lesser German courts, the portraiture nevertheless being just as accurate and attractive. Indeed, in the ceramics collection of the Louvre, where an endeavor has been made to label each individual piece with the principal informative facts concerning it (the make, the date, the modeler or decorator, when known, and, in the case of portrait pieces, the name of the subject represented), there are a considerable number of Paris, Sèvres, Berlin, Saxon and other statuettes labeled *"inconnu."* Thus these pieces are frankly recognized by the museum as portraits, but the individuals they commemorate are "unknown."

The same system is followed in the great museums in Germany.

In a collection of portrait pieces it is almost impossible to avoid having one or more "unknown," or unidentified characters. Hope springs eternal that some day these will be identified and thus claim their proper status in the catalogue. Among my own pieces, I have several which I purchased not knowing definitely whom they might represent, but which I have since accurately and satisfactorily classified. One of these I found in a little New England village. It is a bisque vase about six inches high with the face of a bearded gentleman on either side. The hollow vessel is somewhat in the form of a bust, or rather of two identical busts placed back to back, cut off at the shoulders which form the base. The lip, or mouth of the vase is modeled to represent a wreath of laurel,—which, even when I first saw the piece, led me to infer that I was looking upon the portrait of a poet. And, as I gazed, I seemed to realize that the face was perfectly familiar. I felt as if I had met an acquaintance whose name perversely lapsed from my memory, as so often happens in human intercourse. But with the living one has at least the awkward recourse of apologetically admitting the failure of memory. With a bisque vase, the situation becomes sphinx-like.

It was apparent, however, that this was a poet of modern times. The lapeled coat, the starched collar, the flowing tie, indicated this. I essayed strenuously to conjure to mind the faces of our Nineteenth Century poets, and probably because I was in a New England village, my thoughts were first of American poets,—of Americans with beards,—Longfellow, Lowell, Walt Whitman. I finally concluded, with some misgivings, that here was Lowell; and I paid the modest price demanded by the lady of the shop. When I told her that I thought the vase portrayed James Russell Lowell, she agreed with me at once, and then expressed her annoyance at not having realized this before. She told me frankly she would have charged me more, if she had known the piece was a portrait.

When I got my prize home I began to consider where the piece might have been made. Upon closer examination, I felt some doubt that it could be the product of an American factory. The suspicion and then the conviction came that this was English porcelain. If so, it was probably not a portrait of Lowell. Who could it be then? Who were the modern bearded poets of England? I sought an anthology of English poetry, and had scarcely opened the volume when I knew that my vase pictured Alfred, Lord Tennyson, and that the laurel wreaths were emblematic of his laureateship. Such incidents give zest to portrait hunting.

For a long time, I had on my shelves two pieces, which I could not identify. Recently, by persistent effort, I seem to have determined the portraiture of one of these. Both are jugs; one represents an admiral, the other, a general. The admiral jug with tricorn hat, is cast in the form of a bust cut off at the shoulders. It is of earthenware, decorated in blue and white, and might have been made at Rouen or at Delft or in Staffordshire. The second piece is a puzzle jug, some fourteen inches high, and portrays in half figure and full color a general, or military personage of some sort, a square-jawed, stern-looking individual wearing a Hessian type of headdress.

I have never seen a duplicate of my admiral in any museum, private collection or shop. But I have seen my general twice,—once in London, and once, some twenty years ago, in Ragusa, the last place on earth where I should have expected to uncover a portrait-jug.

The antique or curiosity shops of Ragusa, and other towns in that part of the world, display for the most part Venetian textiles, Byzantine brasses and particularly oriental knives, daggers and pistols of every conceivable variety and design. One might believe that all the brigands of Dalmatia and Montenegro had been shorn of the implements of their trade for the greater temptation of the traveler. And, indeed, this would seem to be a simpler, less brutal, and probably just as successful way of separating the visitor from his money.

In such a shop, on a dark upper shelf, covered with the dust of many seasons, I spied two pottery jugs. When the pantalooned dealer had gotten them down for me, I recognized one as my unknown Hessian General,—whom I now discovered to be one of a pair,—the other representing a noble dame of decidedly teutonic appearance, doubtless the General's wife. I asked the dealer if he knew who was represented by these two jugs. Believing me to be English, he promptly replied that the man was Nelson, the lady his wife. He had probably never heard of Lady Hamilton, or he would have offered a more interesting baptism. I ought to have bought those two pieces, for he offered them at a fair price; but I was traveling light, and feared I should never succeed in getting them safely home. And, besides, I already had the General and did not even know who he was. What could I do with two of him? But I really wanted the lady. She may still be in Ragusa.

My second meeting with the General was in London. One rainy afternoon, as I gazed through the window of a shop in Park Road, I saw the replica of my jug resting on a piece of furniture in the back of the room. My spirits rose, even out there in the dark London rain. Now, thought I, I shall surely find out who he is. I first inquired as to the price of the jug, which was quite modest. I then asked the dealer if he knew who the subject was.

"No," he replied quite frankly; and then with a touch of sadness in his voice: "if I did, I could sell it for twice as much."

"I was hoping you might know who the old boy is," I returned, with equal sadness and disappointment. "I've got him; but I have never been able to find out who he was."

There was immediately a sort of bond between us; we were fellows in misfortune; and I sat down on a Queen Anne chair, and we chatted solemnly, as we gazed out into the drizzle of the street. When I departed, the dealer promised that if he ever learned who the General was, he would let me know; and I promised him the same. I have not heard from him since. And he has not heard from me.

Many dealers realizing that a portrait subject always fetches a higher price than an unidentified piece, do not hesitate to hitch a name to a figure or a statuette, if they think they can get away with it. In a Paris shop one day, the dealer, when he discovered that I was interested in statuettes that were portraits, brought out a porcelain figurine of an imperial grenadier, of which many were made and still are made in the French factories. He represented this to me as a statuette of Napoleon. I pointed out that Napoleon never wore side-whiskers, nor even a bearskin hat.

"Ah," exclaimed the shameless one, "but perhaps Monsieur does not know the story of how the great emperor once found a young soldier asleep on guard, —an offence punishable by death. But Napoleon had a big heart and loved his soldiers. He pitied the young lad, wearied by the long day's march, and instead of calling the guard and ordering the youthful soldier to be shot at sunrise, he took the boy's

H. H. Costain

KING GEORGE IV

Earthenware placque with low relief portrait and impressed inscription "Welcome
George IV," which has been painted over and re-inscribed "William the IVth Britiania."
Size, 5 x 7 inches. Made at Prestonpans, Scotland, 1822. (See page 96.)

ADMIRAL, LORD HOWE

Blue and white earthenware jug. Height, 6 inches. Staffordshire, c. 1790. (See page 107.)

gun and stood on guard in his stead, until the soldier awoke, only to be kindly but sternly reprimanded by his commander. This statuette commemorates that incident; it is Napoleon."

Such an argument was too priceless to be accepted otherwise than in the spirit in which it had been offered. In Rome one must do as the Romans do. Likewise in Paris. So I gazed with admiration upon the statuette and upon the dealer.

"How remarkable!" I exclaimed. "No doubt this piece is one of a pair, the other was the sleeping soldier, and you have not got him—or perhaps he is not awake yet. And how considerate it was of Napoleon to carry about a pair of false whiskers with which to disguise himself as a grenadier."

The dealer who sold me my Admiral, over fifteen years ago, had his shop in West Twenty-eighth Street, New York. He was a more clever and intelligent prevaricator than the romancer in Paris. When I asked who the Admiral was, he replied promptly: "Paul Jones,—a genuine Delft piece."

At that time, I had but the vaguest idea of what Paul Jones looked like, and it was not until considerably later, when I had a better opportunity to examine the piece carefully, that I found it not even to be Delft. But I confess that, at the moment, I accepted both the dealer's statements as true. It was Julius Caesar who said that men easily believe those things which they wish to believe,—*quod fere libenter homines id quod volunt credunt.*

Being perhaps still a trifle skeptical, however, I asked the dealer how he knew this was a portrait of Paul Jones. He smiled, almost patronizingly, and pointed to one of the decorations hanging from the Admiral's neck. This is a sort of circular medal divided vertically down the center by two thin lines, with two other similar lines branching out at angles to the left, making a design similar to an inverted letter K. In the other half of the circle there is a crude design somewhat resembling a star of David. The dealer pointed eagerly to the inverted K.

"You know who Paul Jones was, don't you? The great American sea-fighter who was called to command the Russian fleets, and became a high favorite with the Empress. And you know who the Empress was, don't you? Katherine the Great. That K is for Katherine. This is some decoration she gave him. That proves this is a portrait of Paul Jones."

I was completely hypnotized. But I should have bought the jug anyway, for I knew it was a portrait, even if it might not be a portrait of Paul Jones. It did not take me long, however, by comparing my jug with engravings representing the famous privateer, to decide that there was no likeness here to Paul Jones. The latter had a keen, sharp face, whereas my Admiral is of a full, rotund, rather florid countenance.

It was only recently that his identity became disclosed to me. In my various endeavors to discover who my Admiral was, I sent a photograph to a gentleman in London who specializes in old naval, military and historical pictures. He wrote me that the jug bore an excellent likeness of Admiral Lord Howe; and to make his assurance doubly sure he asserted that the decorations shown on the piece are actually those of Howe.

It is, therefore, most likely that the jug is Staffordshire Delft, for it was in the closing years of the Eighteenth Century that Delft ware began to be quite extensively imitated both at Liverpool and in Staffordshire. Lord Howe achieved his great fame and popularity by his victory over the French fleet, in June 1794, off the island of Ushant. He died in 1799. The jug was probably produced at some time between these two dates.

CHAPTER VIII

N preceding chapters I have referred on several occasions to the Willett Collection in the Public Museum at Brighton. This is to me, in many respects, the most interesting collection of ceramics in England, no doubt because it includes in its scheme an assemblage of portraits in pottery. The collection was formed by Henry Willett Esq., of Brighton, in development of his notion that the history of a country may to a large extent be traced on its homely pottery. It consists of over seventeen hundred pieces, and was gathered during the last twenty-five or thirty years of the Nineteenth Century, the latest dated specimen being a bust of Queen Victoria made in 1897.

The collection is the expression of a novel and interesting idea. Mr. Willett contended that while a piece of pottery might have an interest from its place of manufacture, its design, its maker, its date, its form or its color, all these features were secondary to the leading idea he had in mind which was to demonstrate how the incidents of English life, both public and domestic, have found an expression in pottery.

The collection is divided into twenty-three groups, admittedly arbitrary, but selected with regard to the human interest which the objects represent. The pieces are classified as follows: Royalty and Loyalty; Military Heroes; Naval Heroes; Soldiers and Sailors; England and France; England and America; Statesmen; Clubs and Societies; Philanthropy; Crime; Professions and Trades; Architecture; Scripture History; Religion; Music; Drama; Poetry; Science and Literature; Sporting, Field Sports; Pastimes and Amusements; Agriculture; Conviviality and Teetotalism; Domestic Incidents.

There are 106 pieces in the Royalty and Loyalty group. With very few exceptions these are portrait statuettes, busts and groups; or plates, jugs and mugs bearing portraits of British royalty,—although the earliest of all is not a portrait piece, but a sconce for candles made of yellow glazed earthenware at Isleworth or Hounslow about the year 1600. Upon its face is moulded the royal arms over a Tudor rose, and the initials "E. R."—Elizabeth Regina. The sconce came originally from Hampton Court and there is only one other like it known, which is in the British Museum. Possibly these were a pair.

The earliest portrait pieces are a large Staffordshire Delft dish, of early Seventeenth Century make, decorated with a portrait of Charles I, and a Lambeth Delft plate, of about 1660, with a representation of Charles II in the oak. It will be recalled that Charles, after his defeat at the battle of Worcester, escaped in disguise, and being hard pressed climbed into an oak tree at Boscobel, in an endeavor to

109

conceal himself from his enemies. Another piece, Staffordshire about 1790, a quaintly colored earthenware group, depicts the same incident. There are two pieces picturing Cromwell, both of Staffordshire, one a statuette in color, the other a medallion with portrait in low relief.

There are five examples from the period of William and Mary, four of them portrait pieces, and all dating about 1700. There is a stoneware mug, dated 1721, with a not too complimentary portrait of Queen Anne. Of the five pieces from the reign of George I, only one bears his portrait, the others being gray stoneware flagons and plates with the crowned royal monogram "G. R.," and patriotic inscriptions. Stoneware jugs with "G. R." and the royal crown were made in considerable quantities both at Lambeth and in Flanders, and genuine specimens are occasionally to be picked up even today.

George II is represented by five contemporary portrait pieces, one of which is an exquisite white porcelain bust made at Chelsea and copied from the portrait modeled by Rysbrack.

There are twenty-five numbers associated with George III, the earliest being a Chelsea bust, about 1750, and the latest a New Hall porcelain cup made for the Jubilee in 1809. One of the items is a Staffordshire plate with a picture of the King presenting a Bible to a little girl and saying: "I hope the time will come when every poor child in my dominions will be able to read the Bible." Apparently George

H. H. Costain

THE DUKE OF WELLINGTON

III had no solicitude for the moral training of the offspring of the idle rich.

George IV is represented by only six pieces; but there are nine statuettes, plates, jugs, etc., portraying Queen Caroline, whom he divorced, and seven commemorative of his daughter, the Princess Charlotte, who died soon after she had married Prince Leopold who became King of the Belgians, and whose popularity with the people was so general that a great variety of "mourning" tea sets and other pieces were issued, with designs in black of tombstones and weeping willows and similar appropriate and depressing decorations.

Among the six portraits of William IV, there are two delicate white Derby biscuit porcelain pieces, a bust and a figure seated on a sofa. Curiously enough the collection is wholly lacking in Staffordshire transfer-printed jugs, of which so many were made at the time, portraying William and Adelaide, his Queen.

The reign of Victoria, in which Mr. Willett gathered his collection, is represented by twenty-eight items of which only eighteen portray the Queen, the others relating to her father and her children.

The Naval and Military Heroes include 118 numbers, of which nineteen relate to Wellington and twenty-six to Nelson. The earliest and perhaps among the most interesting, are the four salt-glazed pieces relating to Admiral Vernon and dating about

1740. There are two teapots, a mug and a bowl, all celebrating Vernon's capture of Porto Bello in the Spanish West Indies in 1739. This victory was not a great naval achievement in itself, as the Spanish were entirely unprepared for attack and surrendered to the six English ships without offering any very great resistance. But Vernon's success meant much politically in England. Parliament voted its thanks, medals were struck, and the potters worked overtime. Indeed, it is not impossible, even today, to find one of these salt-glazed Porto Bello commemorative pieces, but they are usually slightly damaged (and no wonder) and the cost is high. Nevertheless a Vernon piece, even in but fair condition, is usually well worth the price demanded.

The Admiral's nickname among his men was "Old Grog." It is generally and erroneously understood that this was due to his having been instrumental in making a radical change in the navy's drink ration. Until his time, the sailors on British ships were allowed a gallon of beer a day; but Vernon, operating in the West Indies, where beer was unobtainable, changed the ration to half a pint of rum per day, giving orders, however, that this be diluted in a quart of water and taken in two doses. This regulation was subsequently adopted throughout the British navy. The nickname "Old Grog" was given to Vernon by the sailors, not on account of his action with respect to rum, but because he wore a peculiar grogram boat cloak. He was called

"Old Grog" long before he established the rum ration. Thus the rum-and-water beverage adopted, and has ever since retained, the name derived from the cloak, exemplifying one of the many instances of the confusion of cause and effect.

The other Eighteenth Century British Admirals are all numerously represented in the collection: Boscawen, Keppel, Rodney, Howe, Duncan, Jervis and Sidney Smith. The fame of the latter rests upon his defense of Acre, in Syria, when England went to the aid of the Turks to resist the invasion of Egypt by Napoleon in 1798. This event was quite elaborately commemorated in pottery, in the form of a jug made in several sizes, of bisque porcelain, or parian ware, with relief groups on either side depicting Sir Sidney Smith standing in the breach of the walls encouraging his men, while Djezzar Pasha, the Turkish commander, seeks to restrain him from exposing himself to the oncoming French. The flags of Turkey and England and the Eagle of Napoleon show clearly in low relief among the struggling soldiers in the background. The Eagle is an anachronism, as Napoleon was not yet emperor, but only a general of the armies of the Directorate. The modeling of the jug is exceedingly well done, even to the minute details of the men's uniforms.

The Nelson pieces form an interesting collection in themselves. There are a number of jugs with portraits of the Admiral and others with grandiloquent verses in praise of his valor. But the most important is a Newcastle jug, the decoration of which, in addition to a portrait and the inscription "England expects every man to do his duty," consists of a detailed annotated plan of the battle of Trafalgar, showing the relative positions of the combined French and Spanish fleets and of the British ships. Fourteen of the twenty-six numbers in this Nelson group were made in 1805, the year of Trafalgar,— concrete evidence of the national enthusiasm which followed this notable event. Only six of the pieces were issued previously, all in celebration of Nelson's victory over the French at the mouth of the Nile.

The Military Heroes are fifty-seven in number, being mostly busts, statuettes and jugs. The earliest examples are two busts of the Duke of Cumberland, one of tortoise-shell ware, the other of Chelsea porcelain, both dating from 1745; a white salt-glazed teapot with an enameled portrait of Prince Charles Edward, about 1750; and a black basaltes medallion about 1780, bearing a bust of the Duke of Marlborough. Mr. Willett includes, among his Military Heroes, Frederick the Great, who indeed was almost as popular a favorite with the British in his day as he was with his own people. The collection includes seven portraits of the Prussian King, one being an exquisite transfer print on a Worcester porcelain mug dated 1757. The Duke of York, second son of George III, is represented by seven items; and Wellington, England's most celebrated military hero, is pictured or alluded to on nineteen. Among the other

114

famous soldiers of whom there are busts or figures in this group are General Wolfe, the Marquis of Granby, Lord Cornwallis, Sir John Moore, General Havelock, and General Gordon. A Staffordshire bust of Florence Nightingale adds to the interest of the half-dozen items relating to the Crimean War.

Among the thirty-one pieces associated with the French Revolution there is a colored earthenware medallion of Marie Antoinette and a pair of tortoise-shell ware busts of her parents, Francis I, Emperor of Germany, and Maria Theresa, the two latter dating from 1760. A blue plate, printed with a picture of the execution of Louis XVI, is inscribed by the ingenuous and loyalist Staffordshire potter: "View of La Guillotine or the modern beheading machine at Paris, by which Louis XVI, late King of France, suffered on the Scaffold, Jan. 12, 1793."

There is a biscuit porcelain bust of Charlotte Corday, but strangely enough the collection does not contain an example of the Staffordshire group showing Charlotte in the act of assassinating Marat. This group, by Lakin & Poole, is excellently modeled and may be seen in several of the more important collections of Staffordshire ware,—as at Hanley, and in the Glaisher collection at Cambridge. History tells us that Charlotte called upon Marat unexpectedly one morning and found him in his bath tub,—which made it comparatively easy for her to stab him. The Staffordshire group, however, shows the girl standing, dagger in hand, while Marat, fully dressed, has

115

fallen to the ground at her feet. Either the Staffordshire potters were not fully informed of the details of the assassination or, the parties to the incident being French, the potters coud not believe the bath tub part of the story.

We have previously noted that Napoleon was, in his own time and even afterwards, the most potted of all historical characters. The Willett Collection contains fifty-two pieces portraying, caricaturing, or satirizing him, from the days of his first consulate until his defeat at Waterloo. All are contemporary, dating between 1800 and 1814. About thirty of them are mugs and jugs printed with caricatures and bearing derisive and scurrilous inscriptions. There are several excellent busts and a porcelain group of "Napoleon Crossing the Alps," modeled after the painting by David.

To Americans, the group listed as "England and America," consisting of some fifty numbers, will perhaps hold the greatest general interest. It is rich in Liverpool jugs, many of which glorify Washington and the colonies' struggle for independence. There are fourteen portrait pieces of George Washington, the most important being a black basaltes bust by Wedgwood. There are six portraits of Franklin; busts of Lafayette and Kosciuszko, and jugs bearing the features of William Penn, Thomas Jefferson, Zebulon Pike, Stephen Decatur, Commodore Perry, Henry Clay, and other noted Americans of that period.

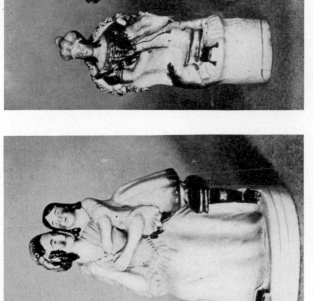

DUCHESS OF KENT AND VICTORIA   QUEEN VICTORIA.   WINDSOR CASTLE.   PRINCE ALBERT.

The group represents the Duchess of Kent with her daughter, Princess, later Queen, Victoria at the age of three.   Staffordshire, c. 1825.   The three other pieces are also Staffordshire, c. 1840.

From the Collection of Miss Edith Feilden

There are not more than half a dozen blue and white plates decorated with American scenes. In fact, in England, there is no representative collection of this tableware. Even the museums at Stoke and Hanley have but a few unimportant specimens.

The section of the Willett Collection devoted to statesmen forms a portrait gallery of high interest, containing many busts and statuettes of rare beauty in themselves. There are several Derby figures, although Staffordshire pieces are naturally in the majority. The earliest example is a Worcester mug, of 1760, printed with a portrait of the Earl of Chatham. British statesmanship is then quite completely portrayed through the reigns of George III, George IV, William IV, and Victoria,—the latest portrait being a figure of Disraeli, made in 1870.

Another large group containing many portraits is that of "Poetry, Science and Literature,"—with busts, figures, placques and jugs representing Chaucer, Shakespeare, Milton, Pope, Burns, Scott, Byron, Longfellow, Locke, Isaac Newton, Defoe, Dr. Johnson, Edward Gibbon, Charles Lamb, Harriet Beecher Stowe and Charles Dickens,—to mention but a few of the most conspicuous. There are sixteen Dickens items, mostly jugs and plates, printed with illustrations from his books. There are half a dozen pieces connected with Mrs. Stowe and *Uncle Tom's Cabin*.

As Mr. Willett's collection was formed with the idea of showing that the history and characteristics of a country are expressed on its homely pottery, it is not surprising that the section devoted to Sports and Sporting should be one of the largest in number and variety of specimens. He makes a sharp dividing line between "sports" and "sporting." The former classification includes shooting, stag and fox hunting, coursing, etc. The latter pictures bull-baiting, bear-baiting, prize fighting, cock fighting and horse racing. An entirely different division entitled Pastimes and Amusements includes such outdoor sports as archery, cricket, riding, bicycling, fishing, dancing, and, curiously enough, ballooning.

In these groupings there are few portrait pieces, although one, of a peculiar and gruesome interest, is included among the Field Sports. It is a colored earthenware group about ten inches high of a man being carried off by a tiger who has the unfortunate individual's head in his mouth. The victim was Lieut. Sir Hector Munroe "an amiable and promising youth," who formed one of a party of British big game hunters who had landed on Sangar Island in December 1792 for jungle shooting. An antelope being reported, some of the sportsmen "rising from lunch, went in pursuit," leaving young Munroe behind. He probably had not finished his port. Came a large royal Bengal tiger, who doubtless had not had any lunch. It promptly sprang upon the young and careless Sir Hector, seized him by the head, and dragged him off into the jungle. The others, hearing the commotion, set out in pursuit, and shot the animal who dropped his victim and escaped. Munroe was able to stagger back to camp, but he had been so frightfully mauled that he only survived twenty-four hours.

I have a pair of lions somewhat similar to this Munroe group, but I have not yet been able to identify the incident they represent. These pieces are nine inches high, resting on bases eight inches wide. They are almost identical in modeling, except that, being a proper pair, one faces to the left and the other to the right. The lions are decorated in white and gold and have an extremely contented and self-satisfied expression of countenance. They are in a seated position, each holding under his fore paws the body of a man, apparently dead, for the eyes are closed. On the other hand, he may be a lion-tamer and he may be sleeping, for his countenance bears a peaceful expression. The man has a dark moustache and goatee, and wears a red coat. In one of the groups he has purple trousers, although not much of these is visible, as the lion is crouching on his legs; in the other he seems to be wearing kilts and a sporran. Up to the present, I have been unable to learn anything definite about these pieces. I have never seen any others like them. I am inclined to believe that they picture some such incident as the killing of a lion-tamer by his own beasts,—a tragedy which would appeal to the sentimentality of a Staffordshire potter, and might

119

very well have resulted in the production of such pieces,—especially if this anonymous potter happened to have been present as a spectator at the traveling circus or menagerie when the tragedy occurred.

Aside from its wealth of portraiture, the Willett Collection is the most extensive and complete assemblage of English folk pottery,—most of it Staffordshire ware,—and a large proportion of that being of the early and mid-Victorian periods. No other museum in England, or anywhere else, so far as I know, has formed any adequate collection of Nineteenth Century Staffordshire cottage pieces. The museums at Stoke, Hanley, Etruria, Liverpool, the Glaisher Collection at Cambridge, the Victoria and Albert Museum, all contain fairly representative collections of late Eighteenth Century and early Nineteenth Century Staffordshire figures. But the curators of these museums, or the collectors who formed these collections, seem either to have ceased collecting, with the accession of Victoria, or to have despised what they may have looked upon as the crude and homely products of the first forty or fifty years of her reign. There is no public collection of Victorian Staffordshire figures and groups, yet no one may deny that these form an important feature of British ceramic development—or stagnation—in the middle years of the Nineteenth Century.

In his preface to the catalogue of the Falkner & Sidebotham Loan Collection of English Pottery

Victoria   Albert   Victoria   Edward VII   Albert   Victoria and Albert

Duke of Cambridge   Victoria and Princess Royal   Victoria   Albert   Alexandra

A GROUP OF VICTORIAN FIGURES OF THE ROYAL FAMILY

Figures, shown at the Royal Museum and Art Galleries, at Manchester, in 1906, Mr. William Burton wrote:

"Everyone with the slightest pretension to a knowledge of English pottery has heard of the china figures and groups made at Bow and Chelsea, at Bristol and Derby. They were made for the gallants and fine ladies of the eighteenth century and have figured in all the chit-chat concerning that age from the letters of Horace Walpole down to the verses of Austin Dobson. Many a charming literary allusion brings to our minds the fashionable boudoir of the eighteenth century glittering with its 'dainty rogues in porcelain,' but no one has thought it worth while to remind us how Betty and Giles loved to bring from the country fair equivalent figures of more homely style and material to deck out their dresser or brighten their mantelshelf. And so it follows that the common rustic figures, made by men who were little more than peasants themselves, have been passed over in silence for the most part, even in ceramic histories."

It may be that the curators and collectors of England are now beginning to awake to the fact that they have been neglecting a period, which, however inartistic it may have been, nevertheless existed, and produced in quantity; for, recently, the Royal Commission on National Museums and Galleries issued its first report, and, among other recommendations, pointed out the importance of forming a Folk Museum, citing the example of the Scandinavian countries, whose collections of arts and crafts of the ordinary people are famous, and admitting that "regrettably Britain has nothing of the kind."

So far as ceramics are concerned, the nearest approach to a Folk Museum in England, at present, is the Willett Collection, at Brighton.

CHAPTER IX

IN England, every business house must remain closed, in addition to Sunday, half a day in every week. This condition results from the Shops Hours Act, and is called Early Closing Day. Every community may determine for itself the particular afternoon on which it prefers to stagnate. In central London,—Westminster, Holborn, the City, etc.,—early closing is on Saturday; in the surrounding districts, it is usually on Wednesday. In provincial towns, as a rule, it is any day but Saturday, probably because in the rural districts this is almost always market day. So important, or, to put it more accurately, of so great a nuisance is this heterogeneity of Early Closing Days that, in most English guide-books and railway time-tables, the Early Closing Days are indicated in heavy type after the name of every city, town and village. Otherwise one is likely to arrive in a town for the transaction of important business, only to find that the entire community is about to shut up shop for the day.

I was in Cheltenham once on Early Closing Day, and found myself looking into an attractive shop window just as the whistles began to blow. Noticing a sudden coming to life and movement among those within, I started to enter with a view to purchasing

123

the object I had been admiring. I was stopped at the door by a determined clerk, who indicated that he was about to lock up the premises. I protested that I wanted to buy something. He replied that it was Early Closing Day, and now already one minute after the hour. I insisted on seeing the proprietor, for I was leaving that afternoon and might never be in Cheltenham again, and I wanted the little dish in the window. Presently the shopkeeper appeared and came out on the sidewalk to converse with me. When I had convinced him that I really wanted to make a purchase, he explained that it would be against the law, and that I must return the next day. Meanwhile, his employees were putting up the shutters and barring the door. At length, however, my persistence prevailed, and the proprietor led me around the corner to a side door through which we obtained entrance to a room back of the now darkened shop. I remained here while he fetched the piece I wanted to see. Our conversation was in low and guarded tones,—it was all reminiscent of bootlegging at home,—and just as hypocritical and ridiculous. But, as a great favor to a lawless American, he sold me the dish, made me conceal it in my overcoat pocket, and then let me cautiously out of the back door again.

During my residence in London, therefore, on Saturdays, I usually took advantage of (or, perhaps better, escaped from) the dull Sunday-like deadliness of the metropolitan district to visit the suburbs, where the clammy hand of Early Closing Day was not throttling the freedom of trade. In unpleasant weather,—and during the winter months, the weather in London is always dark, dismal and unpleasant—I rarely ventured further afield than Chelsea, Hammersmith or Hampstead; but in the brighter and longer days of the better seasons, I visited near-by towns, and even distant cities, such as Salisbury, Canterbury, Winchester,—traveling sometimes by train, sometimes by bus, and occasionally by motor, through that most delightful and picturesque of all countrysides, rural England.

On most of these excursions I was accompanied by a congenial fellow-countryman who was more interested in pewter and prints than in pottery. Thus our desires never clashed; as neither of us ever wanted the same object that the other coveted, which is an essential condition for good comradeship when antiquing in pairs. Another equally important requirement for two who are hunting together is that, in all other respects than their quarry, their tastes shall be as nearly similar as possible. In this we were also fortunate, for we were both interested in architecture, particularly in ecclesiastical architecture (which led us to visit many of the cathedral towns), and we were in especial agreement on the importance of always planning our day so that, at the proper time, we should find ourselves in the vicinity of one of those excellent inns, relics of the old coaching days, of which fortunately there are still some to be found unspoiled.

Our first antiquing adventure beyond the city led us to St. Albans. One may go to St. Albans by train, but we found it pleasanter to travel thither on top of one of the big rabbit buses that start from the Golder's Green terminal of the Underground every twenty minutes, and travel along the Great North Road that was originally built by the Romans, reaching St. Albans in a little over an hour. There is undeniably something thrilling about stepping down from a modern motor bus into what was once the Roman race-course or Verulamium, although at the present day it is but an oblong sunken public square surrounded by little Seventeenth Century houses, and cluttered with market stalls. You may still recognize vaguely the outlines of the amphitheatre, where the raised sidewalks seem to have been built along the upper tiers of the arena seats. But the chief historical monument of the town is the early Norman Cathedral, or Abbey Church, largely constructed of Roman bricks and tiles obtained by the Christian builders from the wreckage that had already been made of Verulamium by the Anglo-Saxons and the Danes.

Almost every cathedral in England claims for itself some exclusive and distinctive feature. St. Albans boasts of the longest gothic nave in existence and, more, that it is the most elevated cathedral in England, which is not really saying much, as it stands but 320 feet above sea level. Salisbury is proud in the possession of the tallest spire; whereas

Lichfield contends that it is the only church in Britain having *three* spires. Exeter is unique in having transeptal towers; Ely has the only gothic dome in existence; Ripon the only early English example of a twin-towered façade; while Wells is conceded to have on its façade the finest collection of mediæval sculpture. York is the largest in area of English mediæval cathedrals; but the Wyckamists point with pride to the fact that Winchester is the *longest* mediæval church, not only in the homeland, but in all of Europe. Chichester's claim to exclusivity is of a somewhat curiously different nature; it has the only cathedral spire in England that is visible from the sea.

No doubt every other English cathedral has some little special and peculiar feature of its very own which tends to make the stranger feel, at the time of his visit, at least, that he is then and there seeing something which no other cathedral can offer. There is merit in this, for, after I had walked the whole length of the nave of St. Albans, I experienced a certain satisfaction at realizing that no other man in all England could achieve in any other place a longer walk down a gothic nave. On the other hand, as I reflected upon this later, my vain sense of superiority was somewhat disturbed by a certain feeling of envy of that comparatively small body of keen-eyed mariners who have seen Chichester's spire from the sea. It is true that, in common with most people, I have admired many cathedral spires from the ground,

127

including Chichester's; but I have never seen Chichester's from the sea. I have seen other cathedral spires from the sea,—San Gennaro of Naples; Sainte Marie Majeure of Marseilles; San Giusto of Trieste; Sant' Anastasia of Zara; Santa Maria Maggiore of Ragusa; the Immaculate Conception of Havana, and perhaps others that I do not now recall. But this is a meagre consolation.

And so, having inspected St. Albans Cathedral, which is, indeed, a most impressive edifice, we wended our way to the Peahen. This pleasant hostelry, dating from the Fifteenth Century, has suffered somewhat from the taste in renovation and interior decoration that prevailed in the Victorian era; but its personality (and inns do have personalities) must have been so strong that even mid-Victorianism, followed by the Twentieth Century plague of automobile tourists, has been unable entirely to rob it of charm, peacefulness and a quaint quality of comfort. Certainly none of the calamities of progress and of the changing times has seemed to affect the standard of its excellent and generous table. Indeed we made several excursions to St. Albans, during the period of my residence in London, lured not so much, I must confess, by the promise of good hunting among the antique shops as by the tempting fare of the Peahen. It is perhaps curious that this should have been so; for the Peahen served exactly the same mid-day meal that is served to the traveler in every inn in all of England. I have visited many, but so far as their

H. H. Costain

PORTRAITS IN POTTERY

bills of fare are concerned, they might all be operating in accordance with some immutable law requiring that they provide soup, roast beef or mutton, boiled potatoes, greens, a sweet and cheese. The greens vary according to season; the sweet, in variety, runs the short gamut of fruit tart, trifle, and plain stewed fruit. No fresh fruit is ever served. In cheese there is usually a choice of Cheddar and Gorgonzola. The Peahen's menu is in no respect different from the national British formula, except perhaps that, if you prefer, you may have delicious cold cuts in place of the roast. This is not unusual in the larger towns.

But the Peahen's soups are wonderful soups; the mutton is of the finest on the Downs; and I am certain that mine host at St. Albans has some private arrangement with the best cheesemaker in the Cheddar valley by which he obtains the choicest cheeses there produced. There is something individual too about the crackers that are served with this cheese, crackers that you might think any innkeeper could provide,—but none other does. And then, there is the ale, that is brewed somewhere near-by, and has a flavor all its own, and is served in pewter tankards whose polished surfaces become dulled and dripping and fogged by the delicious coolness of their contents.

As for antiquing, there are several excellent shops in St. Albans, notably one that is kept by a pleasant lady with whom we eventually became quite well acquainted, and who honored us one day by showing us her own collection in her home. She had some exquisite pieces of furniture, several of which were heirlooms, but others she had acquired from neighbors and townsfolk, who apparently preferred shiny oak to the soft patine of Queen Anne walnut or Chippendale mahogany. She was a very clever woman. She admitted to us quite frankly that she coveted beautiful furniture, but that most fine pieces were beyond her means, until, having ample leisure, she conceived the idea of herself dealing in furniture and of reserving, as her profit, those finer pieces which, in the course of trade, she was frequently able to obtain within the very precincts of her home town.

What particularly attracted me among her treasures was a group of Lambeth stoneware spirit-flasks, many of which were portrait pieces. She had King William IV, Princess Charlotte, Queen Victoria, Lord Brougham, and some others. The sight of them, ranged neatly on the top of a William and Mary lowboy, made me resent that the lady should be a dealer, half a block away, and a collector in her own house. This double life seemed momentarily reprehensible, and it became a great strain upon courtesy to refrain from offering to buy in the lady's parlor, what it would have been perfectly proper to bargain for in her shop. But I did not conceal my keen interest in these Lambeth flasks, and, as a matter of fact, eventually, she was of real assistance to me in procuring several good specimens. At the time, however, it was really almost exasperating to hear her tell of how she had obtained one of hers at a rummage sale for sixpence, and had accidentally found another in a dustbin,—which is the English equivalent for ashcan.

Another town, within about an hour's train ride from London, which attracted us to several visits, is Godalming, a quaint mediæval place with decorated half-timbered Seventeenth Century houses that lean out over the narrow streets in a friendly way, as if bowing to their neighbors opposite. Here we found, in addition to several interesting little antique shops and the hospitable King's Arms, an amiable dealer in furniture, who had a large barn literally packed with chairs, tables, chests, dressers, highboys, lowboys, and what not, that he had gathered out of the jetsam of centuries for miles round about. Among these hundreds of pieces, there were nevertheless many in excellent condition, needing only slight renovation to restore them to their original beauty and usefulness; while others had been so sadly mistreated and so long neglected, that some knowledge of values and considerable faith in the skill of modern craftsmen were required to visualize the treasure that might be developed from the wreck under consideration.

My companion, by tirelessly rummaging among stacks of entangled furniture, and risking his neck in the semi-darkness to dislodge some pieces that hung from hooks in the rafters, succeeded in assembling six oak Jacobean chairs of charming and sturdy design. When we had ranged these on the flagged walk out in the sunlight, we found that all in all they needed but slight repairing and generous rubbing to make them perfect,—and they now serve him in his dining-room at home, together with an aproned table of the same period which he uprooted there on another occasion. We each reclaimed a Seventeenth Century chest from this grimy treasure house, and I retrieved an oak gate-leg table and two wheel-back side chairs. But the greatest find was what looked like excellent material for kindling wood, a mere skeleton of an armchair with a few rags still clinging to it; rags that here and there divulged in faded tatters the secret of their original silken glory. The short walnut legs, however, were comparatively undamaged, and with the sweeping curve of what had once been the upholstered arms, proclaimed the period of Queen Anne. I must admit that, had I been alone, I should probably have overlooked this derelict. But, on this particular visit to Godalming, which had been planned as a furniture hunting expedition, we were accompanied by the ladies of our households,—which proved a good thing for the amiable dealer.

This monstrosity of a backless, seatless armchair was dragged out into the sunlight, where the grime and cobwebs which covered it cruelly emphasized its decrepitude. It was shifted this way and that; it was scratched and pecked at; it was turned upside down and sideways; all its most intimate secrets were investigated and scrutinized. But, in spite of all this, the masculine audience remained callously unenthusiastic, deprecating haste, and pointing out that it would cost ten times as much to rehabilitate this worn out relic as it would to purchase a similar chair in better condition in some other place at some other time. Speeches were then made about the unimaginativeness of mere man, of the folly of procrastination, of the importance of seizing fortune by the forelock, of the futility of believing that there ever would be another time. Vivid word-pictures were drawn of the beauty and the grace which would characterize this Queen Anne chair once it should be scraped, rubbed and upholstered. The ladies decided, even then and there, that it should be upholstered in green.

But apparently the amiable and taciturn dealer, although likewise a mere man, had certain considered opinions as to the value of this particular piece. For, when he was finally drawn from the privacy of his house by the clamor of debate which was going on outside his barn, he nodded wisely and pleasantly and named a sales-figure considerably above the general trend of prices for any pieces we had hitherto pulled out of his storehouse. Be it said in justice, however, he was not the kind of man to profit on enthusiasm,—nor did he ever name one price and accept another. But, as events proved, the chair, even at his price, was almost a gift. And now, as I contemplate it (actually upholstered in pale green damask) the choicest piece of furniture in our living-

room, its lines full of grace and dignity, I concede
that I was justified in surrendering to the inevitable.

So we repaired to the King's Arms and toasted
Queen Anne in old brown sherry; and it was worth
the money paid for the chair to hear the perfectly
frank and unvarnished opinions that were expressed
about masculine sagacity in general, but particularly
with respect to its appreciation of the ghost of an
early Eighteenth Century *fauteuil*.

Not far from Godalming,—less than half an
hour's ride on a bus through one of the most picturesque parts of the Surrey Downs,—is Guildford,
with its broad and very steep High Street, lined with
quaint and picturesque buildings, many of which
house antique shops of greater or lesser merit. To
ransack such was always our avowed object in visiting these several delightful English towns, but frequently we found ourselves neglecting, or missing,
our objective, being diverted from the hunt by less
material considerations which seized upon our interest and usurped our time. For instance, who, when
in Guildford, could resist wandering into the quiet
precincts of Archbishop Abbot's Hospital, founded
in 1619 "to house twelve brothers and ten sisters"
who, in the bodies of a later generation are still there,
peacefully passing their declining years in an atmosphere of all that was good and beautiful in the Seventeenth Century, softened by modern conditions of
comfort and ease, and brightened by this year's
flowers that bloom so gaily in the quiet little court-

yard? Who could resist climbing to the top of the keep of the Twelfth Century Norman Castle in the public gardens, or refrain from strolling along the banks of the placid Wey, where lovers in punts idled beneath the drooping willows? We could not. We neglected some of the antique shops to sit in a little tea garden by the river, and on our return to town we paused for a brief moment at the grave of the author of "Alice in Wonderland."

And so it was that Guildford, too, attracted us more than once; and more than once we fared well at The Angel; and eventually we fared well in the antique shops, where I found several historic jugs and a brave little Staffordshire figure of Macbeth.

But it was not by any means always that I returned from these rural excursions with a parcel under my arm. On the contrary, more often than not I came back empty-handed,—but never without the recollection of some cheerful incident, some kindly word in passing, or with the memory picture of some quaint little village,—some mediæval church,—some rural vista,—all of which now cluster about and glorify the more concrete trophies of these pleasant adventures.

On some occasions, indeed, we planned our wanderings more for the pure enjoyment of the great outdoors than for the chase of the elusive antique,— confident nevertheless, that any countryside we might visit would unfailingly provide one or more opportunities for us to indulge in our favorite avocation. It was on one such outing that we laid our course through Amersham, Chalfont St. Giles, Stoke Poges, Eton and Windsor.

Amersham lies some twenty-five miles to the northwest of London, in Buckinghamshire, about an hour's train ride from Marylebone Station. It is an old coaching town, now left to crumble in its memories, for the stream of travel and commerce has been diverted to the railway, and the little station for Amersham lies over the hills more than a mile from the town. It was here that we stepped down from the somnolent little local train one fair spring morning and set forth across country afoot, tramping along the winding road between blossoming thorn hedges, with the steeple of Amersham church rising as our guidemark against the brilliant greens of the Chiltern Hills beyond.

The village consists almost entirely of one long and extremely wide street, bordered by half-timbered houses, built in the reign of William and Mary. They needed wide streets in those days for a coach and four required ample space in which to turn about. But today, these broad open spaces are accentuated by the total absence of traffic. The occasional wayfarers seem to cling to the houses, as if danger lurked in the great deserted thoroughfare; even the dogs skulk in the shadows of the overhanging gables. The inhabitants seem to while their time away in the making of chairs of the Windsor type,—for Windsor lies not far to the southward, and the chair industry

A. C. Shaw

LAMBETH AND ROCKINGHAM FLASKS PORTRAYING VICTORIA AND ALBERT

is carried on in the cottages and villages for miles roundabout. I suspect that much of this handmade furniture, the work of skilled and honest craftsmen, finds its way into the back shops of less conscientious London dealers, where rottenstone and stain, and a little rough handling convert many of these Windsor chairs into saleable antiques.

We strolled from one end to the other of Amersham's long street, loitering for a while in the courtyard of the quaint Elizabethan almshouse, and nearby found two little antique shops where friendly old ladies awoke hopefully to our entrance, but were as disappointed as we were at the result of our visits.

The roast lamb at the Crown was crisp and juicy, and the Watford ale was up to standard. The little paneled dining-room was hung with faded prints of the coaches that had brought prosperity to Amersham in the past; but grass was growing among the stones in the inn yard.

So, presently, we climbed to the top of a big motor bus that had heaved into the quiet little village from the outside world. With a grinding of gears it lurched into a narrow by-street, and then out upon the winding highway that leads to Chalfont St. Giles. Here again we came to earth, for we could not pass heedlessly on when within but a stone's throw of the house where Milton had lived in 1665, and where he wrote the final lines of *Paradise Lost* and began *Paradise Regained*. The little thatched cottage, with its vines and flowers, must still appear quite the same as it did when the poet lived there. Nothing has changed much in Chalfont St. Giles. The trees probably cast denser shadows, and there may be a little more moss on the bricks in the walls.

We stood for a moment in Milton's room, and pictured him at his task:

"They, hand in hand, with wandering step and slow
Through Eden took their solitary way."

And then:

"I, who erstwhile the happy garden sung,
By one man's disobedience lost, now sing
Recovered Paradise to all mankind . . ."

while the black plague raged in London, whence he had fled. We thanked heaven that there was no black plague in London today, and pensively found our way again to the highwayside, where we waited until another rural bus came along to jolt us back into the Twentieth Century, and carry us commonplacedly Londonward.

As we rolled through Stoke Poges we glimpsed the Country Churchyard made famous by Thomas Gray in his Elegy. But we did not pause to do homage to the poet's memory; for we, too, from our bus-top, beheld "a Distant Prospect of Eton College," and the sun was already well bent upon its downward course. Our objective was Windsor, but as the bus wound its way slowly through the streets of Eton, we were beguiled from our determination by the beck of many antique shops. We abandoned our howdah and took to foot.

It was quite unexpected, and really in the nature of a surprise, to come suddenly upon so many alluring windows, and to find the shops so well stocked and so metropolitan in their general appearance and arrangement. We knew there were quantities of antique shops in Windsor, that mecca of tourists across the river,—but we had not given any thought to the possibilities of Eton.

Yet the explanation was quite simple. We were in an academic town, and such towns, the world over, so far as my experience goes, are usually lavish in the display of wares that appeal to the cultured and well-to-do. In our own country, there are excellent antique shops in New Haven, Cambridge, Hartford, Princeton and other college towns. In England the same condition holds true for Oxford and Cambridge, and indeed for Eton, Harrow and Winchester, where there are great schools.

Upon slight reflection it becomes apparent that a college town offers one of the best of markets for wares of quality and merit. Not because of the students, very few of whom have probably as yet awakened to a sense of tasteful acquisition, but because of the standard of culture which characterizes the entire community.

A large proportion of the dwellers in college towns are directly or indirectly connected with the institution of learning which gives the place its importance. They are people of education, refinement and taste, if not always of wealth. But, in addition to these, you will also invariably find many families of ample means who have chosen to make their homes in the academic quiet and restful atmosphere of scholastic surroundings. Such residents give to any community an enviable standard of citizenship. Furthermore, at all times during the year, and in great numbers at certain festival periods, the families and friends of the student body contribute a floating population by no means to be left unconsidered.

We spent an hour or more in Eton's attractive antique shops, and when we walked across the bridge to Windsor, I stepped carefully, for I carried a statuette of John Wesley under one arm and a Queen Adelaide portrait-jug under the other. At the far end of the bridge, we turned into an inviting gateway, and presently found ourselves in a little tea garden by the edge of the river. There we rested and drank tea and looked out upon the quiet flow of the Thames, where swans floated in pairs unmindful of the many skylarkers in punts and hired rowboats. We gazed in admiration upon enthusiastic young men in pair-oared racing shells, and imagined they were noble young Etonians practicing for the crew, whereas, in all probability, they were but drapers' assistants from Slough, where Saturday is Early Closing Day.

CHAPTER X

HE cathedral towns within easy access of London are Canterbury, Chichester, Winchester, Salisbury, Rochester and St. Albans, of which I have already spoken. In all these places there are many antique shops, and in each one of those towns I added one or more notables to my gallery of portraits in pottery. In Salisbury I was particularly fortunate in finding not only a well-modeled group of St. George and the Dragon, but a fine little statuette of the historian Edward Gibbon, and a quaint, brightly colored, early Victorian pair representing the young Queen holding baby Prince Albert Edward in her arms, with the Prince Consort as companion piece, erect and dignified, wearing an expression of countenance such as any young father might proudly assume.

Indeed, our excursion to Salisbury was one of the most enjoyable of my English adventures. We went there in July, and, for England, the day was actually hot, although clear and dry and with a bracing atmosphere. We spent the morning in and about the cathedral which, to me, is the most imposing and beautiful of those I had the opportunity to visit in England.

It is different from all others in that it was built

on a virgin site especially selected for the purpose, and not erected upon the ruins of some lesser ecclesiastical edifice, as most English cathedrals were. Thus it stands in a great greenswarded space, its dignity and grandeur unimpaired by the encroachment of dingy tenements. Majestically set in its tranquil close, it is framed by low, neat, graceful buildings and noble trees.

Nor is Salisbury Cathedral an architectural patchwork as so many other cathedrals are. For Bishop Poore, early in the Thirteenth Century, decreed "Let us have a cathedral,"—and forthwith set upon the task. In less than forty years, under his own supervision, the magnificent edifice was completed to the exact design that was originally laid down for it. Unfortunately, some three hundred years later, just about when the interior was mellowing toward perfection in wealth of sculpture and monumental decoration, a too orderly minded young architect named Wyatt,—unrestrained if not actually encouraged by George III,—removed the screens and chapels and rearranged the monuments and tombs in tidy rows, —which caused Motley to observe that Salisbury was too neat. On the other hand, Henry James, being a gentleman with preferences, described Salisbury Cathedral as "a blonde beauty among churches." I agree with both Motley and James, and, for the sake of courtesy, reserve my opinion of Wyatt.

When, all too soon, the hour came for consideration of the inner man, we found our way to the

VOLTAIRE

White jasper bust on a round black basaltes pedestal. Height, 4¾ inches. Josiah Wedgwood, Etruria, c. 1780.

J.-J. ROUSSEAU

Colored earthenware bust from the portrait by Laval. Height, 6½ inches, by Enoch Wood, Staffordshire, c. 1800.

Schreiber Collection, Victoria and Albert Museum

ADMIRAL DUNCAN

Drab stoneware bust of Admiral Lord Adam Duncan, Viscount Camperdown. Height, 8¾ in. Liverpool, c. 1800.

Schreiber Collection

BONAPARTE

Colored earthenware bust of Napoleon as he appeared when First Consul. Height, 10 in. Staffordshire, c. 1802.

Willett Collection

market place and sought the Haunch of Venison, quite the most fascinating little pub that hungry wanderers could wish to fall upon. The tourists who throng into Salisbury patronize the greater inns, where snorting motors block the fairway, and vitiate the atmosphere. The Haunch of Venison is patronized by leather-putteed, red faced, jovial men; and the tiny bar is tended by two of the prettiest girls I saw while in England.

The fiction that barmaids are pretty, and saucy, and quick of wit, had long since been dispelled in my mind. Those I had seen in London and otherwheres all had the appearance of being genuine antiques, and many, I am sure, were grandmothers. But these two Wiltshire lassies were rosy and young and quite of the type presented in mid-Victorian novels by the shameless imaginists of that period. On the other hand, it is possible that, in those times, all London barmaids actually were young and beautiful,—and, in addition, possessed of such sturdy health and vitality that these same barmaids have held their jobs even until today. The *prima facie* and all other facial evidence would seem to lend support to this theory.

It was in my mind to discuss this matter with the two fair barmaids of Salisbury, adopting this tactful method of expressing my admiration for their own comeliness. But, although I made a determined effort to wedge my way through the milling phalanx of native admirers which blocked the narrow passage

143

to the shrine of beauty and beer, I was eventually compelled to desist of my purpose, and shall therefor never know the real quality of their rippling wit.

We climbed a narrow, winding stairway, to the chop-room above, where a waiter who might have stepped from the pages of Dickens received us with a dignity and cordiality in full accord with the hospitable atmosphere of the place.

We ate crisp radishes, and thick Southdown chops, and bright emerald peas. We drank cool, cool ale,— for it was really a hot day. But when we asked for fresh fruit, the attentive waiter apologetically replied that there was none such. We exclaimed that the market, which we looked upon from the window where we sat, was full of cherries, currants, raspberries and pears. He freely admitted this so evident a fact, but assured us with earnestness, that all fresh fruit was cooked as soon as it came into the house, lest some part of it should spoil. We found this to be true in all the English inns we visited.

So we paid our score and wandered again into the market place where we each bought a large bag of luscious cherries. We sat under a great tree, upon a broad stone bench, and playfully shot the pits at friendly pigeons which gathered about us, and seemed flutteringly astonished at our unseemly behavior.

In the late afternoon we boarded a motor bus for Amesbury, where we slept at the George; and the next morning we chartered a horse-drawn vehicle of

early Victorian design and drove two miles to Stonehenge. We considered this primitive method of approach to be much more in keeping with the spirit
of the occasion. There seemed to us something incongruous about swooping down upon these prehistoric trilithons in what the Druids would probably
have looked upon as a devil wagon. And as we stood
in respectful contemplation of those great stones, my
companion called my attention to the fact that they
were probably the most genuinely antique antiques
that we were likely to see in all our travels.

Canterbury Cathedral, in spite of its more important historical background, was of lesser interest
to me than Salisbury; and Canterbury Town was a
disappointment in so far as its antique shops were
concerned. There are many such shops in the city,
but so great is the number of visitors constantly
attracted there by the fame of the cathedral, that
these shops are pretty well combed of their portable
articles of interest. It would be a mistake, however,
to conclude that Canterbury—or any other place
similarly tourist-thronged—is hopeless and void of
opportunity for the antiquer. I have known of some
good pieces, particularly chairs, to come out of Canterbury. But for smaller objects,—pottery and glass,
—the coincidence of chance is the major factor of the
hunter's luck.

At Winchester, on the other hand, we found very
good hunting, and there I was so fortunate as to
acquire a Queen Caroline cream ware jug with the

portrait and decorations applied in relief in a delightful tone of blue, and a colored Parian figure of Havelock, most exquisite in its portraiture.

At Chichester too, there are several worth while shops, and The Dolphin is an excellent inn. One may sit there at a window in the coffee room and look up at the slender spire of the cathedral directly opposite, —a spire which, as we now know, is the only one among the cathedrals of England that is visible from the sea.

In the immediate neighborhood of Chichester are several delightful little towns in every one of which some small window sparkles with tempting bits of lustre, or glass, or old silverware. At Midhurst is the Spread Eagle Inn, probably considerably restored, but in actual appearance just about as it looked in the days of Queen Elizabeth, who used to spend an occasional week-end at Cowdray Castle, near-by. The castle today is a magnificent ruin, surrounded by a well kept park, where tame deer feed peacefully, unconcerned with the riot of the rising generation of Midhurst. In the days of Elizabeth the deer, with good reason, were not so tame; for the Earl Cowdray's idea of entertaining his royal guest was to organize a great hunt in the forest, then surrounding his Tudor mansion. It is told that at these Elizabethan hunt breakfasts, the guests thought nothing of consuming "six oxen, forty bucks, ten suckling pigs, twenty sheep, sixty rabbits, forty brace of

146

MARQUIS OF GRANBY   GENERAL WOLFE

A pair of porcelain figures from the Willett Collection. Height, 14 inches.
Bow, *c.* 1760.

JOHN WILKES   FIELD MARSHAL CONWAY

A pair of porcelain figures from the Metropolitan Museum Collection.
Height, 11¾ inches. Chelsea, *c.* 1765.

wildfowl, as many roasted geese and three hogsheads of beer."

As for ourselves, in this Twentieth Century, when appetite has become degenerate, (unless we choose to contend that it has become refined), we were well content with the comparatively simple fare at the Spread Eagle where, nevertheless, a whole pheasant was placed before us. We ate in a room whose high pointed ceiling was upheld and crossed by great beams that were no doubt hewn in the very forest and in the very days that Elizabeth satisfied her dainty appetite at Cowdray Castle. And, in another room of the inn, beamed and paneled too, was an antique shop where I captured a jug bearing a portrait of King George IV.

Not far beyond Midhurst lies Petworth; and then Arundel, and Grinsted and Horsham. In all of them there were, and no doubt still are, little treasures to try the resisting powers of the most callous. As I recall to mind these many quiet villages into which my wanderings led me, little incidents in each one of them seem to pop up out of the rusty recesses of my memory,—pleasant trifles which momentarily assume a charm seemingly worthy of record. Yet, as my rekindled enthusiasm prompts me to grow loquacious, it suddenly occurs to me that, after all, such minor phases of a day's progress can have but a privy importance; and, as a penny held before the eye appears to display a greater circumference than the dome of St. Paul's, so those amenities, which touch me thus closely, tend perhaps to deprive me of that sense of proportion which, like a sense of humor, should be an ever present talisman against garrulity. Yet, I hesitate to muzzle my enthusiasm completely, for in these random notes the patient reader may perchance find certain indications of value. And so, for a brief space, my theme is still of towns easily and comfortably accessible from London as a day's adventure.

We found Portsmouth interesting, although it had no great number of antique shops. But at the Old London House, a pub not far from the dockyard (where the "Victory," Nelson's flagship at Trafalgar, may still be visited), we were delighted with a display of ship models, and came very near to burdening ourselves with a three masted full rigged ship. Apparently, the ancient mariners of the neighborhood have adopted the London House as a sort of clearing house for their products, for a dozen or more models of the "Victory" were available there at prices by no means excessive. These models varied in size and in quality of workmanship, but they made a brave showing along the walls of the tap room, interspersed here and there with brigs, sloops, and even modern torpedo boats.

Southsea adjoining Portsmouth, is actually the residential section of this great naval base, and is a fashionable watering place as well as a favorite residence of retired naval and military officers. For both these reasons, as we have similarly observed with respect to college towns, Southsea is a fertile field for the antiquer.

Retired naval officers may properly be counted among the traveled and the cultured; many of them are scions of old families whose heirlooms have fallen to their heritage. With retired naval officers, as with all men, a time comes when their earthly treasures are dispersed. And so it happens that in Southsea one may frequently find rare objects of interest and value,—furniture of the best English periods, curious weapons in great variety, old maps, oriental pottery and jades, Indian embroideries and Persian carpets.

Another town, in some respects similar to Portsmouth and Southsea, in that there is also a great dockyard there, is Chatham. Rochester and Chatham are such near neighbors as practically to form one town, with one long winding principal street in which the antiquer will find a variety of shops to his liking,—although the average is by no means so high here as at Southsea. Another good combination for a day's adventure are Dover and Folkestone, in each of which there is good hunting.

Oxford and Cambridge, in the opposite direction from London, may each fairly well be antiquely explored in one day, but it is preferable to devote a little more time, if possible, to these famous university towns. After all, one does not go to Oxford or to Cambridge primarily to hunt antiques. Their monuments and their historic associations are so overshadowing as to give our hobby but a secondary importance, in spite of the fact that opportunity lurks almost everywhere in the byways among the colleges.

The shorter trips indeed, if we are considering antiquing adventures as the main object of these excursions, are the most amusing, the more casual and usually the most profitable. For it is quite easy to bring back one or two pieces if the journey homeward is short and direct; but it is not so easy to transport one or more parcels of perhaps fragile booty, if the return journey happens to be complicated by changes of transportation methods at the crowded hours of the day's end. Thus towns like Richmond, Hampton Court, Epsom, Farnham, Maidenhead (they still have some good Hock left in the cellar at Skindle's), Sevenoaks, Tunbridge Wells, Hitchin, Beaconsfield, Reigate and Dorking, to instance but a few among many, are easily accessible suburban localities well worth visiting. And even if you return empty handed you will surely retain a pleasant recollection of the luncheon hour at the inn.

At Richmond you must stop for tea and eat "Maids of Honor," a sort of sweet cheese cake originally devised and named for Queen Caroline's ladies of honor. At Hampton Court, there is the palace to distract you for the major part of your day, but there is also The Mitre, famous for its peas and ducks. At Sevenoaks there is Knole, one of the finest baronial mansions in all England; and at Tunbridge Wells,

150

only a little way beyond, you stroll where Beau Brummel strutted, in the Pantiles, with countless antique shops to be found in all the neighboring little streets.

At Dorking there is the White Horse, straggling and black timbered, but still retaining the charm and hospitality characteristic of the old coaching inns. Next door is a shop with a windowful of decanters. At least such was the case upon the occasions of my several visits to this quaint village; and if what the shopkeeper said was true, the decanters are no doubt still there. I had never before seen so many decanters together; many of them were highly desirable specimens of old English glass. My curiosity led me to inquire of the proprietor of the establishment how it came that he had so great a number and variety of bottles. He had many other things too, but he appeared to be a glutton for decanters.

He appeared depressed at my inquiry, but explained that in the past he had found that American visitors to Dorking were much more likely to buy decanters than larger or heavier objects less easily carried away. He had therefore made it a point to acquire as many decanters as he could find in order to cater to this American trade,—when all of a sudden the Americans adopted Prohibition, and now they don't buy any more decanters. Thus does the pernicious influence of the Volstead law reach far beyond the seas to paralyze the antique trade in Dorking.

151

CHAPTER XI

F all places in the world, London is unquestionably the richest field for the collector of antiques and the searcher after curios and objects of virtu. There are more antiquaries, more art dealers, more junk-shops, more opportunities there than anywhere else. I believe, provided sufficient funds were available for the purpose, that even today, any expert connoisseur could assemble in London a collection of almost any character, whether mediæval or even oriental, of ivories, arms, furniture, pictures, porcelains and jewels, to equal many of the most famous private collections already in existence. For the collector of modest means, London is still an unexhausted gold mine.

The shops where these treasures may be discovered are more or less grouped in districts. The higher class dealers in exquisite and rare objects of art are located almost exclusively in Mayfair; whereas the smaller and less pretentious, although in many cases very excellent shops, are scattered in clusters throughout every section of the metropolitan area. While I occasionally visited the larger establishments, for educational and æsthetic reasons, more than with any idea that I might there discover anything within my means, I spent most of my available time in ferreting

John Evelyn Collection

Schreiber Collection

WILLIAM SHAKESPEARE

The figure on the left is of Chelsea porcelain, height, 12½ inches; the one on the right, of Staffordshire earthenware, height, 18½ inches. Both pieces, c. 1800, were modeled after the statue in Westminster Abbey, made by Peter Scheemakers, from a design by William Kent. Around the lower part of the pedestals are busts of Queen Elizabeth, Henry V, and Richard III. Scheemakers' statue was executed in 1740 and inspired many other sculptors. Enoch Wood also made a figure from this same model.

out the possibilities of the more distant side streets, —with the result that, in a period of a little over a year, I confidently believe I covered a very considerable portion of London on foot; and through those streets which I did not walk, I rode on top of a bus.

As a result of these explorations I obtained a pretty good idea of which localities provide good hunting, as well as of those which are devoid of any interest to the antiquer. It may prove of value to other collectors if I give here a brief survey of those sections and streets where they will be certain to find many shops worth inspection.

Those more pretentious establishments, which classify themselves as galleries for the sale of antique objects of art, will mostly be found in Bond Street, St. James's Street, Duke Street and King Street, where Christie's famous auction rooms are also located. There are similar high-class shops in the shorter side streets of this neighborhood, such as Ryder Street, Albermarle Street, Bruton Street, Grafton Street, and others. The orientalist should visit King Street, where also, in another shop, may be found the most beautiful of Eighteenth and early Nineteenth Century English porcelains and decorated dinner services. For old English silver, Ryder Street. For old English glass, Bond Street; and likewise in a less pretentious little shop, tucked away in Shepherd's Market, off Curzon Street. For sporting prints and jugs, for armor and Eighteenth Century toby-jugs, Duke Street. Period furniture, paintings

153

and tapestries, may be seen in many shops throughout this quarter, particularly in St. James's Street.

For the collector of average purse, however, the less central districts of London offer much greater interest and adventure; and none of these favorable localities are more than twenty minutes walk or bus-ride from Piccadilly Circus. Even in that immediate vicinity, Wardour Street presents many opportunities, and Charing Cross Road is a perfect paradise for book collectors. Moving eastward we see an occasional shop in Longacre. Crossing Kingsway, we find better hunting in Portugal Street, passing on the way, in Portsmouth Street, the spurious "Old Curiosity Shop" of Dickens, where many deceive themselves daily in misguided contemplation of a house that Dickens probably never even saw. Continue through Lincoln's Inn Fields and follow the wall northward to Great Turnstile. This is a narrow little paved alley leading into Holborn, and it contains several excellent antique shops. A couple of blocks eastward, along Holborn, and we come to the gabled and timbered façade of Staple Inn, which shelters a curious little hole-in-the-wall well worth looking into. Retracing our steps along Holborn for a few blocks we turn into Red Lion Street, and presently find our way leftward through a paved alley into Red Lion Court, where several other similar alleys converge from various directions. There are likely antique shops in most of these.

In Theobald's Road, beyond, there is also good

hunting; and, in the neighborhood of the British Museum, a few blocks westward, there are a dozen or more shops, almost in a row. Many little streets running into New Oxford Street will be found to contain the kind of shops one is looking for; notably Silver Street and the little square at the end of it. Great Russell Street, Broad Street, High Street, Shaftesbury Avenue, all near by, contain shops of a greater or lesser merit.

Another district not far from Piccadilly Circus, but in an opposite direction, includes Wigmore Street, George Street, Orchard Street, Baker Street, Park Road, and the many byways of that general neighborhood. Baker Street is a particularly fertile field. In Park Road is one of the best shops for pewter in all London.

The Edgware Road, running northward from the Marble Arch, opens up a rich district for the antiquer. Praed Street, which leads out of this avenue to Paddington Station, is full of likely places. The streets around Euston Station are also worth exploring. In all these neighborhoods the minor crossways should not be neglected.

Further westward is the Notting Hill section. To reach this easily and quickly, a good method of procedure is to take the Underground to Notting Hill Station. When you come up for air, you will find yourself almost wholly surrounded by antique shops, second-hand furniture shops, dealers in ship models, brokers and the like. Having canvassed the streets within a radius of a quarter of a mile, set your course down Church Street toward Kensington. To visit thoroughly all the antique shops in Church Street would require several days. On reaching Kensington High Street, you may turn east or west with no fear of being disappointed in either direction. But in Knightsbridge, and southward from there, is one of the best of all hunting grounds in London.

The Brompton Road forks out of Knightsbridge at the Knightsbridge Station of the Piccadilly Tube, which is an excellent starting point, as there is an antique shop right there in the Tube arcade. The Brompton Road and its tributaries are literally packed with antique shops of every kind and quality; and when you have finished with these you may continue into the Fulham Road, where there is equally good hunting, although of a slightly inferior and diversified quality.

Beyond Westminster Abbey, Victoria Street and Vauxhall Road offer many opportunities. At Victoria Station, cross Grosvenor Square into Ebury Street where there are half a dozen good shops. Continue westward to Sloane Square where there are more; then proceed along the King's Road through Chelsea where the pickings are even better.

Chelsea is that part of London where many artists and literary folk have chosen to make their homes, and where the struggling younger painters, sculptors and writers seem to prefer to live. Artists travel; they wander to the far and strange places of the earth;

they like beautiful things and they possess taste.
When they return they bring with them the trophies
of their adventure. Sometimes, alas, the lean years
follow, and the first things to be sacrificed to an unkind fate are those luxuries which may be, or must be,
bartered for necessities. Thus the second-hand shops
of Chelsea become enriched, and consequently here
the curio hunter is likely to find objects of great
beauty and great value. The West End dealers are
well aware of this, and they frequently forage in
Chelsea.

Across the Thames lies Battersea, where there are
a few shops with possibilities; but, generally speaking, there is little favorable territory on the Surrey
side of the river. In Battersea, as everywhere else,
one should be extremely wary of the fascination of
those dainty little enamel boxes,—most of those
offered for sale today (not only in Battersea, but
anywhere) being of recent French manufacture. My
experience is that few English dealers deliberately
proffer these as antiques; but, on the other hand, not
many go out of their way to inform the eager buyer
that they are modern reproductions. The antique
shops of Paris are full of them,—"bought from an
old English collector who died here recently."

In North London, Hampstead offers another
promising field for investigation. The best way to
get there is to take the Tube to Hampstead Station.
Here on Heath Street and High Street, within a comparatively small compass, there are several shops,

and more will be found on the return trip to Westminster by walking back either down Finchley Road
or Haverstock Hill. Other neighborhoods, where one
is not likely to search in vain, are Chiswick, Hammersmith and Shepherds' Bush.

But the most fascinating of all hunting grounds
in London is the Caledonian Market, in the north-
eastern section, at the top of the Caledonian Road.
It is easily reached by taking the Underground to
Caledonia Road Station, or by bus. Its official designation is the Metropolitan Cattle Market, because, on
Mondays and Thursdays, markets for the sale of
sheep and cattle are held there. With its buildings it
occupies an area of some fifty acres, but the paved
open spaces, which interest us, are probably about
twenty acres in extent. Here, on Fridays (and recently on Tuesdays as well, but Friday is the best
day) from ten in the morning until four in the afternoon is held the "peddlars' market" or "rag fair,"
where all kinds of second-hand wares are offered for
sale, from rusty iron junk to period furniture.

It is well to attend the market as early as possible,
as there are always great crowds of buyers with eager
eyes for desirable bargains. Upon issuing from the
Underground, you walk a distance of a few short
blocks to the gates of the great iron fence which sur-
rounds the market. You then find yourself in a vast
stone-paved enclosure, divided into streets or thoroughfares by the low-fenced pens which, on other
days, are used for cattle. But, on Fridays, these pens

(which have been thoroughly cleansed overnight) and even the roadways, are occupied by the pedlars who spread their wares on the pavement, or display them on barrows (meaning push-carts), or in little temporary booths, or under canvas. For the most part, however, even glass, pottery, laces and silver-ware are merely laid out on old carpets or blankets spread on the stone flagging.

At the Caledonian Market you will find antiques and semi-antiques and curios of every conceivable kind, in every state of repair and decrepitude. Where all this stuff comes from is a mystery; but it comes, nevertheless. There is nothing I can think of that is not offered for sale at this place, not even excepting diamonds. There is old silver and plated ware in great quantities. I never could overcome the feeling, in looking about me at half an acre of silverplate, that a number of the houses of the rich must certainly have been robbed the night before. It is startling to see porcelain and delicate glass lying about on the roadway, or being quite carelessly handled by a motley multitude of bargain hunters who, for the most part, appear to have no appreciation of either. I shall never cease to wonder how all these frail pieces are packed and repacked and transported without disaster, for at many of the stalls I have seen pieces that I had noticed before, which indicates that they must have been carried back and forth to the market several times.

But, as at all such bazaars, *caveat emptor*. The

Caledonian is full of fakes, impostures and imitations. Yet, mingled with and hidden among these are the priceless nuggets worth digging for.

In most cases the dealers know the worth of their wares, and stiff bargaining is usually necessary. In many cases, however, they are wholly ignorant of values—and here lie the opportunities of the connoisseur. Many collectors of my acquaintance go to the market regularly every Friday. Sometimes they find nothing; at other times they fall upon some gem. Dealers go there in considerable numbers. Adventurers in possibilities and treasure hunters are always there,—for more than once, in the past, genuine treasures of considerable value have been discovered at the Caledonian.

On a Friday, in August 1925, Mr. C. J. Pool, a dealer whose shop is in the City, visited the Caledonian Market as was his weekly custom. He had been doing this for years, and frequently gathered up from the coster stalls objects suitable for his trade. On this particular occasion, while rummaging over a barrow loaded with a variety of decrepit furniture, lighting fixtures, grates, shovels, and other household wreckage, he noticed two terra cotta busts. He retrieved these and examined them rather carefully. They were in perfectly good condition and seemed well worth the modest price of seven shillings and sixpence which the coster demanded for the pair.

Mr. Pool had no special knowledge of sculpture, and did not recognize either of the portraits; but the

THE CALEDONIAN MARKET, LONDON

(See pages 158-164)

busts appeared to him to display certain qualities of merit, particularly as one of them was signed. So he bought them on the chance that they might be worth somewhat more than the few shillings he was willing to risk on their purchase. Not knowing what would be a fair price to put upon them in his shop, he went a few days later to the British Museum, in an endeavor to identify the pieces, and carried along with him one of the busts wrapped in an old newspaper. As is usual, when an inconspicuous citizen approaches officialdom, Mr. Pool experienced some difficulty and delay in obtaining access to the expert authority he was seeking. However, while waiting in one of the Museum's halls for an opportunity to display the object of his solicitude, he suddenly noticed, with a thrill, among the casts ranged about the room, what appeared to be a plaster replica of the very bust he had brought along with him. When, at last, the pleasant lady who is the British Museum's expert in matters of Eighteenth Century sculpture, came out to see him, he was even more thrilled by her surprise and delight at discovering that his was none other than the original bust of Milton modeled by Roubillac about 1750, of which all trace had been lost for nearly two hundred years.

In the reign of George I, William Benson succeeded Sir Christopher Wren as Surveyor-General of the Buildings of the King. At that time, two of the most famous Eighteenth Century sculptors, Roubillac and Rysbrack, were working in London. Rou-

billac was of French birth, but lived the greater part
of his life in London. There are many of his sculptures in Westminster Abbey, and his statue of
Shakespeare, commissioned by David Garrick, stands
in the British Museum. Rysbrack was Flemish.
Much of his work is likewise preserved in the Abbey,
notably the Isaac Newton memorial. Benson was
perhaps a pompous person, but he had a genuine love
of literature and the arts. He became a patron of
both these sculptors, and it is of record that he
ordered from Rysbrack a bust of the great Scottish
Latinist, Arthur Johnston, and that he acquired
from Roubillac a terra cotta study of Milton's head.
At Benson's death many of his art treasures passed
to his daughter, and are still in the possession of her
descendants; but the busts of Milton and Johnston
were not among these. A plaster cast of a bust of
Milton was found in Roubillac's studio after his
death,—which implied that the original had passed
into the hands of a patron. This cast was purchased
by Dr. Maty and presented to the British Museum
in 1762. A careful examination of the British Museum's cast has proven conclusively that it was made
from the terra cotta bust found by Mr. Pool. The
bust of Johnston is signed by Rysbrack, with the
date 1739. Both terra cottas are mounted in the same
manner, on plain wooden stands. Of their fate between the days of Benson and August 1925, when
they were discovered in the Caledonian Market,
nothing whatever is known. Mr. Pool, as well as the

British Museum authorities, endeavored in vain to trace their mysterious career. All that could be learned from the Caledonian pedlar was that he had bought, from an obscure dealer in East London, a job lot of second-hand furniture and house furnishings. This obscure dealer remembered having obtained the busts, with other job lots, at an auction; but all the auctioneer could recall was that the goods he sold had come to him from many different junk-men and second-hand dealers, losing their identity and all record of their antecedents as they were dumped into the auction rooms.

It is a marvel that the busts remained undamaged throughout their peregrinations. Not only do they seem to have been companions for nearly two centuries, not only are they admirable works of art, but, as was written by the eminent authority who identified them, "they have the distinction which no other Eighteenth Century terra cottas can claim, of being visible annotations of the passage in the *Dunciad* in which their enthusiastic owner is unfairly pilloried. More than ever we see poor Benson with the eyes of Pope:

" 'On two unequal crutches propt he came
   Milton on this, on that one Johnston's name.' "

Mr. Pool's finds were eventually purchased from him by the Scottish National Portrait Gallery, of Edinburgh, where they are now preserved. For his acute judgment and small investment of seven shil-

lings and sixpence, he received £150—about $750.
This was a good day's work. I asked Mr. Pool if he
had ever had any other similar good fortune at the
Caledonian Market, which he attends every Friday.
He said he had made one other lucky find. This was
a painting of the head of a man, which seemed to
him to have unusual qualities. He bought it for three
shillings, say seventy-five cents. It proved to be a
portrait of Sir Herbert Tree by John Sergeant, and
Mr. Pool sold it for fifty guineas,—about $250.

CHAPTER XII

ONDON is in every respect a city of strong and striking contrasts. Wealth and poverty, the past and the present, beauty and ugliness rub elbows at every hand. Little slovenly districts lie in the shadows of the greatest mansions. Academic quiet is a neighbor to the raucous clamor of Fleet Street, and may be found by merely stepping through an archway into the groved yards of the Temple.

Quite in tune with this condition, there are, in what might be called the gilt-edged district of St. James's, one or two small antique shops of an entirely different character from the elaborate galleries that predominate in those select thoroughfares,— little dark holes cluttered with that usual confusion of disassorted castaways. Here, the collector must do his own hunting amid dust and litter. Here he may find the odd tumbler to complete his set, or the cut glass stopper to fit his gaping decanter, or the saucer to match the widowed cup he has so long hesitated to discard. Or, indeed more, he may come upon some really delectable item in the line that his fancy follows.

Crown Court is a narrow little alley that runs through from King Street to Pall Mall, issuing directly opposite Marlborough House. One enters it through a low and inconspicuous archway alongside St. James's Theatre. The place is dark, damp, and crowded with smelly little cubby-holes where cigarettes and fruit are for sale; greasy lunch counters about which the porters and messenger boys of the neighborhood congregate to munch curious morsels at all hours of the day; cobbler shops, a small stationer, a dismal barber shop, and the like. In the midst of this mess, with misty windows, and only a flickering gas jet to light the mysterious interior, there is a little antique shop, where, on various occasions, I have found good hunting. It was there that I uncovered a delightful little bisque statuette of King Edward VII, in full regalia, modeled and signed by Geflowski, a late-Victorian sculptor of some repute. It was of a dull gray hue when I picked it from a tray of assorted and maimed remnants of chinaware. I paid one-and-six for it, which is thirty-six cents. When I got it home, I scrubbed it in warm water and soap, and, thus purified, I set it up before a dark background, against which the dignified and graceful little figurine stood out in all the soft white purity that is the seductive charm of bisque.

I have frequently wondered why so many of the smaller dealers fail to appreciate the importance of properly presenting their wares. A little soap and water, a little elbow grease, would so often seem to make it possible for them to realize double or treble the price they accept for some unclean, but otherwise undamaged piece. It is not because they lack the time

POPE LEO XIII

Earthenware portrait-jug modeled
by J. S. W. Starkey. Height, 8½
inches. East Liverpool, O. 1892.

ADMIRAL NELSON

Saltglazed stoneware jug. Height,
7½ inches. Doulton & Watts,
Lambeth Pottery, London. 1820.

JOHN BROWN

Earthenware group, from the
Willett Collection. Height, 10¾
inches. Staffordshire, c. 1860.

OOM PAUL KRUGER

Decorated terra-cotta tobacco jar.
Height, 13 inches. Probably
produced in Germany, c. 1900.

to put their house in order, for how often do we see them reading last week's paper in the half-light of the back shop, or standing idly in the doorway, gazing blankly into the street, or even dully dozing in a far corner while possible customers hesitate to enter for fear of disturbing their quiet. Yet such is the nature of these gentry. Perhaps, without them, there would be something lacking to the zest of antiquing.

However, the Crown Court dealer of whom I am speaking was not at all of this indolent character, in spite of the fact that his goods were motley and neglected. On the contrary he always appeared somehow to be busy in a dark closet, under the stairway which led to his quarters above. I imagine he bought odd lots at small auctions, or took over bankrupt stocks, or acquired trunks and bundles that were sold for storage charges,—for he seemed forever to be searching and sorting in boxes and parcels, trying to fit small parts to greater parts, puttering, and puttering, and puttering. He always had a courteous greeting for anyone who entered his shop, but after that you could wander about and uproot anything in the place, unwatched and undisturbed. He had a clientele, and occasionally he would talk to me of certain of his customers. On one occasion, when I seemed to be interested in a Rockingham cow creamer (which unfortunately had a broken horn and was consequently *vacca non grata* to me) he told me of one of his clients, an elderly gentleman of wealth living in the Albany, the most exclusive bachelors' chambers in London, who had a collection numbering more than five hundred cows, mostly ceramic, but including some of silver, pewter and glass. I expressed an eager desire that some way might be devised between us by which I might see these cows; but, although the dealer appeared sympathetic to my interest, nothing resulted.

On another occasion, when I had bought a Lambeth portrait-jug of Nelson, and had asked him if he would not keep on the lookout on my behalf for similar jugs, he confided to me that he already had another customer, a retired Captain of the Royal Flying Corps who collected Lambeth jugs and flasks, whom he always notified when he had a piece of that type. He painted such a fascinating picture of this collection of Lambeth ware that I almost begged him to let me know when he next anticipated a visit from the Captain, so that I might casually drop in and perhaps make acquaintance with him, and possibly be invited to visit his collection. I fully realized that there was about as much chance of a retired British Army Officer unbending to the extent of inviting a mere stranger to visit his collection, as there would be of the Archbishop of Canterbury asking me to come down and pry into the shrine of St. Thomas à Becket. And so I was not particularly concerned at never hearing again of the retired Captain of the Royal Flying Corps, and soon relegated him and the cow-gentleman of the Albany to that

gallery of probably mythical characters the principal
of which is the well known "American lady" who, I
was so frequently told, had been in the shop only
about an hour before, and had purchased the very
object I might be looking for.

I crossed the trail of this American lady many,
many times. On certain occasions, however, the collector who had just taken what I wanted was an
American gentleman, and once she was a Lady-in-
Waiting to the Queen. This was at Eton. They
have plenty of imagination at Eton,—and, besides,
Windsor is only just across the river from there,
and so, *perhaps,* I did almost step on the heels of a
Lady-in-Waiting. It is not well to be too skeptical.

Indeed, in collecting, fact is actually frequently
stranger than fiction. For it was in this very same
little shop in Crown Court that I observed, late one
afternoon, my friend the dealer in close and subdued
conversation with an elderly gentleman wearing
horn spectacles and a trim gray beard. They had
some small object under examination, which they
passed back and forth to one another, and looked
at critically through a magnifying glass. I could not
make out exactly what the object was; but it was
small and blue and might have been an ushabti. At
any rate, the spectacled gentleman bought it, shook
hands pleasantly and walked out into the dark, wet
alley. As the dealer tucked some crumpled banknotes
into his waistcoat pocket, he observed to me, with a
certain superiority:

"That's one of the gentlemen from the British Museum."

This remark thoroughly convinced me that Crown Court was the home of romance, and that this dealer's little world was peopled with curators and rich collectors, and perhaps princes and fairies, who came into his dark shop and bought treasures that the eyes of the casual visitor were far too dull to discern.

Yet, not long afterward, I had occasion to visit the ceramic collection in the British Museum. To reach this section, you may walk either through the Egyptian Galleries or through the King's Library. On this occasion, as chance would have it, I passed by way of the Egyptian rooms, where there were very few visitors, and I happened to notice a gentleman, assisted by a uniformed attendant, apparently arranging some small objects in an opened showcase. The gentleman wore horn spectacles and a trim gray beard, and the stoop of his shoulders was reminiscent. I looked more carefully, as I passed nearer, and recognized the customer of the Crown Court shop.

And so my gallery of mythical characters was depleted of at least one celebrity. But I was rather pleased, for it restored my faith considerably in human nature, and perhaps in dealers, generally. The world seemed a more interesting place to live in, if it should indeed be true that it is peopled with curators and retired army captains who can find treasures in back alleys. There must then be hope and opportunity for lesser gleaners.

Not alone in Crown Court, however, did I cross the trails of seemingly fictitious or of actually existing personages. Once, in a section of London which ever delights me by its picturesque designation of Shepherd's Bush, I almost laid hands upon the elusive "American lady" who, so many times before, had just forestalled me of my quarry. In the course of an afternoon's wandering, I had come upon a small shop in the window of which, among countless other things, stood a Staffordshire figure of a horseman. The grime and moisture on the panes made it difficult to determine from without anything more than the general outline and color of this statuette. I could merely see that the figure represented a bearded man, wearing a brilliant red coat, mounted on a pink horse.

I have often wondered what the reason can be which has prompted so many of the Staffordshire potters to create pink horses. I asked an English friend about this once. He replied that that part of England where the potteries are located is called the Black Country, because its climate and its coal and its furnaces pretty well deprive it of its normal allowance of sunlight. A white horse, in the glare of the kilns, actually looks pink. I pass this explanation along for what it may be worth. Possibly it is a real contribution to the pigmentology of ceramic art.

171

However, to return to this particular pink horse of Shepherd's Bush. I wanted to examine him more closely; but a lady was standing at the window apparently likewise fascinated by the brilliant cavalier. I hoped she might presently satisfy her curiosity and proceed upon her errand. But, instead, she entered the shop.

This gave me an opportunity to draw closer, and to note that the figure probably represented Garibaldi. As I was endeavoring to appraise the merit of the piece, an arm stretched forth from the darkness beyond, and a grimy hand lifted Garibaldi out of my ken. I felt a flush of resentment, realizing at once that the lady had inquired about the statuette, and even now probably held it in her hands. I had come along just a few minutes too late. The statuette immediately acquired great beauty and value in my estimation. What a fool I had been to waste my time outside, peeking through a dirty windowpane, when I might have gone straight on in and captured the prize! I was now certain that it was a prize. I gazed morbidly at the vacant spot in the show case. Then, suddenly, I had the consoling thought that perhaps the lady would not buy Garibaldi, after all. On the other hand, she might. Pink horses hold a great attraction for women.

I decided I should see the thing through. I would wait until the lady came out of the shop, and if she had not bought Garibaldi, I should go in and take a look at him myself. But, on the other hand, if the

McKinley   Lincoln   Roosevelt

H. H. Costain   Washington   Garfield   Lincoln   Washington   Hoover

PRESIDENTS OF THE UNITED STATES

lady captured the prize, and presently appeared in the doorway, radiant, with a parcel under her arm, what should I do?

I walked across the street, and like the villain in a melodrama, I stood in the conventionally flickering light of a street lamp,—for it gets dark early in London in wintertime, and, in Shepherd's Bush, they still have gas lamps to light the lesser thoroughfares.

It took this lady a long time to make up her mind. At least it seemed so to me. Or else, it took the dealer a long time to wrap up the parcel. Or else perhaps the lady was not interested in Garibaldi, and was now poking about among the usual miscellany of such a shop.

Suddenly I heard the tinkle of the warning bell that hangs on the door of every little antique shop in London. I looked up and saw the lady stepping out into the street. She carried a parcel under her arm, and I could tell from its size and general awkwardness that it contained Garibaldi. I was torn with conflicting emotions, just as any villain in a melodrama should be. The lady, wholly unconscious of my presence, or of my villainous humor, tripped blithely on her way; while I, after a brief hesitation, followed in her wake. What should I do? Should I stop her and ask her to let me have a look at Garibaldi? Should I ask her how much she paid for him? Yet, if I spoke to her, she might scream and have me arrested. I thought of how awkward it would be to get arrested for accosting a lady in Shepherd's Bush.

173

Then, all of a sudden, as she passed under a light and I got a good look at her, I realized she was an American. Another shock. Here, at last, was the American lady! So it was all true. There *was* an American lady who picked up the good things just ahead of me. I thought I ought to stop her and reason with her, even if I did risk being arrested; and I had the wild idea of suggesting that in the future we go hunting together, or that we delimit the territory, or that we toss a coin, or something . . . and, as my mind worked wildly, she faded into thin air, or turned a corner, or entered a doorway, or was swallowed up by the earth. At any rate, she disappeared; and I stood on a corner, like a fool, looking in every direction, to no purpose.

Perhaps other collectors know how it feels to have something you want literally lifted from under your very nose. It is much the way the bull must feel when the slippery matador wafts the red shawl away, just as he thinks he is about to hook it. The bull rages and snorts and paws the earth. I could have done the same. But, instead, I turned about and decided to go back to the shop and inquire in a casual sort of way, what the price of the figure was that had stood in the window that day.

When I reached the place, I hesitated for a few moments and stood gaping at the vacant space, where only a few minutes ago the pink horse had made so brave a show. As I stared, an arm reached forward from the darkness again, and the same grimy hand carefully placed in the original position a red-shirted rider on a pink horse. I thought I must be dreaming. I rubbed my eyes, and pressed my nose again close to the pane. It was certainly Garibaldi; if not the same Garibaldi, at least one exactly like the first. My feeling of resentment toward the American lady melted away. I began to suspect, with unkind glee, that perhaps I might not have missed a prize after all. Presently I even chuckled; and upon obtaining proper control of myself I entered the shop. The dealer was a shrewd looking old party of unclean appearance.

"How much for the chalk horse?" I snapped at him, jerking my thumb toward the window.

"That's no chalk horse," the man retorted; "that's Staffordshire."

"Oh," I exclaimed in surprise; and with an intonation of apology: "Then it is not what I am looking for. I want three or four of those figures; must all be alike, and pretty cheap."

"I can let you have three like that one at seven-and-six each. I've been selling them at fifteen shillings. What's your game?"

"Raffling," I said. "That's more than I can pay. Thanks just the same. Good-night."

I heaved a sigh of satisfaction as I found my way slowly toward the Tube station. I had verified my suspicion. Garibaldi was a dud. Like many another Staffordshire statuette today, he may be bought by the dozen. The potteries sell these reproductions in good faith as modern reproductions, but I cannot see how they can fail to realize that unscrupulous dealers palm them off as original pieces. And, as I pondered, I began to feel,—as I had frequently suspected,—that the tales of the American lady's prowess are probably no more genuine than the piece my American lady had purchased that day.

I have still another association with Shepherd's Bush, which, however, is not to me so amusing as my fruitless chase of the American lady. For it was likewise in that quaintly named part of London that I missed two opportunities. Collectors always like to boast of the lucky finds they have made, of the prizes they have captured through their astuteness, or by virtue of what they like to consider their superior knowledge. But few of us like to tell of our mistakes, of our failures, of our indecisions, of our very ignorance when any of these was the cause of missing a good thing. Yet confession is good for the soul,—and I certainly did miss two good things in Shepherd's Bush: one through indecision,—the other through ignorance.

I had been wandering about that part of London one winter afternoon, and finally stumbled upon a little shop which displayed in its windows several pieces of pottery among an assortment of miscellaneous modern objects, such as laces and purses, strings of beads, glass and porcelain vases, little boxes, and an infinite variety of similar objects. The place might perhaps best be designated as a neighborhood shop, of which there are many in these outlying parts of London. To such shops the heirlooms and bric-a-brac of the district seem to gravitate, as their original owners move away, or feel the necessity of realizing on some small object which they can convert into cash. Thus, in such places, mixed with the modern and apparently useless mass of stock in trade, one frequently happens on an interesting and desirable item.

In this case, I was attracted by a stoneware tobacco-jar modeled in the form of a square, squatty house, the chimnied roof forming the cover of the jar. Across the front, in underglaze impressed lettering, were the words "RYE HOUSE." I went in and looked at Rye House. It was an interesting piece, a well-designed little model in good condition, and obviously not of modern make. I asked the young woman, who subsequently proved to be the daughter of the shopkeeper, what the words "Rye House" meant. She said she did not know. I asked her if perhaps it might not be a jar made to advertise a distillery, as nowadays one sees everywhere, jugs, pitchers and ash-receivers flamboyantly proclaiming the merits of certain whiskies, ales, or cigarettes. At the moment, it did not occur to me that this form of publicity was extremely modern, and wholly out of tune with the period in which the tobacco-jar must have been produced, and so, with carelessness and inattention, added to complete ignorance concerning Rye House, I set the jar back on its shelf.

Next, I looked about the shop, and soon noticed on the far wall two oval earthenware placques, about six inches high. They were portraits of Eighteenth Century personages, a man and a woman. They were very simple in design, the portraits being modeled in low relief of a soft cream color on a light blue background. The glaze was excellent, and with the exception of a few insignificant time or fire cracks, the pieces were in fine condition. The portraits represented George III, whose reign began in 1760, and Queen Charlotte. I desired at once to possess them. I estimated from the portraiture that the placques must certainly have been made in the early lifetime of both the King and the Queen, who died in 1820 and 1818 respectively. It would be unlikely that such companion portraits would be produced after the death of these rulers. The appearance and the feel of the pieces justified the assumption.

I asked the price. It was immediately apparent that the young lady's father had some idea,—it seemed to me an exaggerated idea,—of the value of these placques. The sum she mentioned was about double what I had thought I should be willing to pay, and I had not expected to get them cheap. I tried to bargain with her; but she protested that only her father could make any reduction. I ought to have paid the price and taken the treasures; but, instead, I told her I should think the matter over and come again some time when I could discuss terms with her father.

APOSTLES JUG

Buff unglazed stoneware. Height, 9 inches.
Charles Meigh, Hanley, 1842.

Metropolitan Museum

H. H. Costain

UNCLE TOM'S CABIN JUG

Grey unglazed stoneware. Height, 7 inches.
Ridgway & Abingdon, Hanley, 1853.

(See page 83.)

When I left the shop it was dark, and somewhat foggy. I asked the first police constable I met to direct me to the nearest Underground station, which proved to be several blocks distant and rather difficult to find, as I had to ask my way once again from a passer-by.

As soon as I got home, I checked up the George III dates in my English History, and, then, on the mere chance, I took a glance through the index to see if, perhaps, there was any historical association connected with Rye House. There certainly was. I quickly discovered that it was in the Manor House of Rye, situated on the River Lea, near Hertford, that Colonel Rumbold and his followers hatched the infamous "Rye House Plot" for the assassination of Charles II and his brother James, in 1683. The plot failed, Rumbold fled the country, but was afterwards taken and executed. Rye House was partly demolished some two hundred years ago, but fragments of the original manor still exist as portions of an inn, which is today a favorite haunt of fishermen. At Hoddeson, not far from there, stood Izaak Walton's Old Thatched House. Today, one of the great attractions of the inn, which consists partly of the original old Rye House, is the famed Great Bed of Ware, large enough to accommodate twelve persons, and alluded to by Shakespeare in *Twelfth Night*. Truly in collecting pottery, one stumbles upon queer bits of interesting information.

I doubt very much if the Rye House tobacco-jar

was a product contemporary of the period in which the plot stirred the countryside. However, it might have been; for Dwight began making stoneware in 1671, and other potters were producing it commercially in 1690. My impression is that the Rye House tobacco-jar I saw in Shepherd's Bush was of a considerably later date of manufacture.

For, toward the latter part of the Eighteenth Century, and afterward, it was quite customary with many of the inns to have their names stamped on stoneware jugs and spirit flasks. Whether the innkeepers had these made to sell or give away, or whether they were stamped as a protective measure against the souvenir hunters of that epoch, I cannot say. I have a stoneware flask that was probably made about the time of Nelson, decorated with a low-relief group of a sailor and soldier in the costumes of the period. On the back is impressed "Sowter, Queen's Head, Brompton, Kent." I have seen other flasks with the impressed names of other inns. If inns had their names impressed on flasks and jugs, why not on tobacco-jars as well? This would seem to be a more reasonable explanation, and would date the tobacco-jar approximately as of the time when the inn on the River Lea was built up around the ruins of the dismantled Rye House, say 1800 or thereabouts.

Thus, I was considerably annoyed with myself for not having picked up the tobacco-jar, particularly as the price asked was only five or six shillings.

True, it did not come exactly within my scheme of collecting, but nevertheless it was an unusual piece that would prove a very desirable acquisition to any collector of cottages. By cottage collectors, any piece representing an historical building, or bearing a name or a date, is most highly prized. There are very few such models. In the Willett Collection, at Brighton, there are only four: Westminster Abbey, the Red Barn at Polestead, Potash Farm, and Stanfield Hall. The last three were associated with notorious crimes in 1828 and 1848. There is no Rye House in the Willett Collection. There were probably very few Rye House tobacco-jars made.

Among the London dealers with whom I had become acquainted, there was one in Great Turnstile, who always had a number of cottages on his shelves, which would seem to indicate that in his clientele there were collectors of this type of pottery. A couple of days later I stopped in to see him and told him about the Rye House tobacco-jar. He was much interested, and knowing that I was not a collector of cottages, he said that if I cared to make an exchange, he would be quite willing to take over the Rye House jar at the equivalent of one pound, provided it was as I had represented it.

Now, this dealer had a transfer-print portrait-jug which I had long coveted, but the price of which, —a guinea—had seemed to me a bit steep, although it was an excellent piece. I saw here, then, the opportunity to obtain this prize by an exchange which would bring the cost of the jug down to five or six shillings. I consequently decided to go out to Shepherd's Bush again at the first possible opportunity, and not only retrieve the Rye House jar, but the portrait placques of George III and Queen Charlotte as well, even if I had to pay the price, for I concluded that as the latter were unquestionably of late Eighteenth Century make, I must not allow them to escape me by further indecision and delay.

It was not, however, until the following Saturday that I was able to resume my quest. It was another dull, dark day, but I set forth gaily and with confidence, and emerged from the Tube at the station I had taken, homeward bound, the week before. I started in the direction from which I thought I had come, but very soon realized that I did not remember very distinctly the turns and twists I had previously followed. I reproached myself for not having made a note of the street and number of that shop. Nevertheless, I persevered, and wandered hither and yon with persistence and determination. I did this futilely for two hours or more, and when for the nth time I found myself back again at the Tube station, wearied and worn, I abandoned the search for that day.

Fully determined, however, not to be baffled, I resumed my exploration the following afternoon, starting this time from where my first excursion had originally begun, in an endeavor to follow my first trail, instead of working along the back track. The more I wandered, the more confused I became. As

182

evening fell, I had not yet found the shop,—and I never have found that shop, although I made two brief attempts on subsequent occasions. This seems hardly credible, but it is true. No doubt some other collector, who knows what he wants when he wants it, and hesitates not when opportunity offers, now possesses those placques and the Rye House jar; and while I envy him their possession I bear him no resentment, for I lost them by indecision and ignorance.

It is plain that the well informed collector frequently picks up valuable pieces that have escaped the attention of others, possessed of a smaller store of miscellaneous information. Yet, no one, however well informed, may hope never to miss anything. It would take a human encyclopedia to be familiar with every historic association and attribute of the thousands of objects that come to the notice even of the most casual antiquer. Value, after all, is relative, so far as collectors are concerned. A Rockingham statuette of Lord Rodney would immediately arouse my keen interest, and would have great value in my estimation; whereas a collector of oriental jades would pass it by without even looking at it. I should probably overlook the jade, although it might be unique, and almost priceless to one familiar with the qualities and values of jades.

I found, however, that most Englishmen have a very broad knowledge of the history of their own country, even to minor details, and of events that would seem to be only of local interest in distant places. The average American knows very little about the history of his own country, and apparently cares less. I found I could learn a great deal from the English antique dealers, most of whom are extremely well informed, and invariably amiably eager to impart information to one who shows an intelligent interest in his subject.

However, while there may be some excuse for ignorance on the part of a stranger in a strange land, as in the case of my encounter with Rye House, there seems to be little excuse for indecision. When hunting for antiques, or any other quarry, one must make quick decisions, after naturally giving due consideration to values. Mistakes will occasionally be made; but, in antiquing, it is perhaps wiser to make mistakes of commission than of omission. And, in antiquing, too, it so frequently happens that opportunity comes but once. True to form, it always comes unexpectedly. It also usually comes in places where one is never likely to be again,—in little towns where one has stopped over for a train connection, in a village along the route of a motor-trip, in distant or out of the way localities, or even in Shepherd's Bush.

All of us, who have pursued the sport of collecting, have at times, for one good reason or another, decided "to think it over," before buying some object that has attracted us. In many cases, we have finally decided not to make the purchase; and I should say that more often than not, no regret follows. But

KING FRANÇOIS I

Porcelain inkstand brilliantly colored.
Height, 8 inches. Old Paris, c. 1810.

Collection of M. de Brunhoff

ROBINSON CRUSOE

Elaborately colored porcelain figure.
One of a pair, the other being Friday.
Height, 5 in. Rockingham, c. 1825.

KING LOUIS XVI

QUEEN MARIE ANTOINETTE

A pair of bisque busts on blue enamel pedestals. Height, 12 inches. Sèvres, 1820.

Metropolitan Museum

there is always a certain risk in delaying to reach a decision. It is a psychological fact, which many dealers have confirmed to me, that when one person becomes interested in some piece,—even one which may have been in the shop for a long time, unheeded by anyone,—it very frequently happens that one or more other customers suddenly develop an interest in the same object, and it is sold.

CHAPTER XIII

NTIQUING in France is not nearly so entertaining or resultful as it is in England. There are perhaps just as many antique shops of the average type, but their offerings are for the most part of little merit or value. There are not so many interesting towns scattered about the suburban district of Paris, as there are in the neighborhood of London. The motor roads out of Paris are wretched stone-paved highways, passing through sordid and dreary communities. The suburban railway service is dilatory, dirty and expensive.

Thus the antiquer in France will find his best opportunities in Paris—and that is not saying much, —or in the larger provincial cities. He will find practically nothing in the villages or small towns, except perhaps along the Channel coast, where the great number of summer visitors from England seems to have inspired a few enterprising junkmen to gather such copper pots and farmhouse furniture as they could persuade the peasantry to part with.

Revolutions, invasions, and the national characteristic, which may politely be described as thrift, have been the contributing causes to this dearth of material in today's antique markets in France. A noted French author and collector, M. Paul Morand, thus accounts for the curious difference between conditions in England and France: "The Englishman, alternatively extravagant and needy, parts with everything that he does not consider absolutely necessary. The Frenchman never relinquishes anything. He uses his belongings until they are threadbare, and puts by in the sepulchre of his great rustic closets all that he does not need. He absorbs everything and gives back nothing. This explains why French markets are so disappointing. One could apply to them the African dialogue between the young hyena and its mother. The young hyena found a bone and went to show it to the mother hyena. The latter said: 'Has your father seen it?' 'Yes.' Then the mother hyena replied, 'If your father has seen it, you may as well throw it away. There is nothing left after that.' "

Nevertheless, in Paris and in provincial France, for certain things, there is still good hunting,—but you *must* hunt. And you must be extremely wary. The average French antique dealer has no pride of craft, and is shamelessly mendacious. Fakes, imitations, and forgeries abound; and the French swindle one another as cheerfully as they swindle a stranger, as has been fully exposed in the writings of M. Edmond Haraucourt, formerly director of the Musée de Cluny, in Paris. He has pointed out many spurious pieces, not only in the national museums of his own country, but in many great private collections. He says: "The further south we travel, the greater the number of frauds. The more we approach those countries where imagination is overheated by the sun, the more often we are liable to encounter those pretended historic souvenirs."

He refers particularly to Italy and to Spain, in both of which countries the forgery of antiques amounts actually to an important industry. I have been told, by a man who has actually witnessed the performance, of a swindle which is still carried on in a little town in central Spain,—in Don Quixote's country,—as frequently as opportunity affords.

In the little church of that town, there is an altar painting by Greco. It is a blue Madonna, and a very desirable painting. Not infrequently some touring American millionaire,—in person, as he covetously admires the painting, or later on, through a subsidized native representative,—expresses a fervent desire to own this painting. He is willing to pay many thousand pesetas to obtain it, in spite of the fact that it is contrary to Spanish law to sell or export any art treasure. The deed can be done, however. There is a very capable artist who, for a consideration, would paint a copy of the Greco Madonna, and this copy could be substituted for the original over the altar in the church, in the little out of the way Spanish town.

It would cost certain thousands of pesetas to do this,—but it could be done. There are negotiations, and the deal is closed. The copy is ordered. At length it is finished. The purchaser sees it, and marvels at the excellence of the reproduction,—age-cracks and all. At least, he thinks he sees it. What he is looking upon, however, is the original, the copy having previously been placed in the frame above the altar.

The purchaser comes at night, leaving his motor waiting in the quiet village square. He is present in the dimly lighted church, when the Greco is tenderly taken down from above the altar; and, as his heart throbs wildly, he sees it replaced with the "copy." He pays his thousands of pesetas, and goes on his way to smuggle the canvas across the border.

My informant tells me that, to his definite knowledge, the Greco has been sold and carried away seven times; and yet the original still hangs in the church. Its custodian considers himself a very clever man, and is perhaps justified in believing that many rich collectors are fools. One or more of the owners of the blue Madonna by Greco from the church of Santa M— may perchance read these paragraphs and be edified.

However, while Paris is not quite as far south as Spain, it is yet far enough south for the imaginations of fakers and forgers to become overheated by what little sun shines there. Honesty, after all, is not a matter of latitude. It is more a matter of attitude; and the Frenchman's attitude toward honesty is much like his attitude toward woman. Thus we must have no illusions when pursuing the antique on the Continent. Yet, there are certain types of things which may still be found there to great advantage, and Paris is indeed an excellent place in

189

which to pick up furniture, mirrors, chandeliers, clocks, miniatures and prints.

My personal taste does not incline to French furniture. I do not admire the gilt and brocades of the Louis periods, and I see no beauty in the gewgaws of the heavy Napoleonic styles. A Louis XIII chair follows somewhat the lines of its contemporary English furniture, and has more character than any of the later French designs. But a genuine Louis XIII chair is hard to find today. Reconstructed pieces, with perhaps one genuine leg or arm, are not particularly rare. But most of the furniture offered for sale in the Paris antique shops, except in the elaborate establishments of the Place Vendome and the Faubourg St. Honoré, is of the first empire and thereafter.

Books and prints may be found in great quantities,—although many of the latter are reprints. In spite of what Mr. Morand says about Frenchmen never relinquishing anything of value, my observation leads me to believe that they are not all hyenas so far as their books are concerned,—for the second-hand book market of Paris is certainly glutted, and good editions of French books, often in fine bindings, are obtainable quite cheaply.

The principal second-hand book market is on the quais along the left bank of the Seine,—Quai Voltaire, Quai Malaquais, Quai Conti, Quai St. Michel,—extending for about a mile from the Pont Royal, which spans the river at the western end of the Louvre. The quai walls, for this entire distance,

SECOND-HAND BOOKSTALLS ON THE QUAIS ALONG THE SEINE, PARIS

are covered with heavy wooden boxes of a generally uniform design (each about the size of an ordinary steamer trunk), which the city rents to the dealers. By day the lids of these boxes are lifted to display the wares; at night they are closed and padlocked and left where they are,—firmly clamped to the granite wall.

Some dealers have but one stall, but most of them have at least two, while others have as many as four, —which affords them an opportunity for quite an effective display. In addition to books, there are great quantities of prints, engravings, lithographs and maps. One may occasionally find good prints and good maps, but the majority of those offered are modern reprints. It is amusing, sometimes, to observe the disingenuousness of these sidewalk dealers, when several of them, within but a few stalls of one another, display identically the same "rare Seventeeth Century map" or "unique Eighteenth Century print." And yet, not infrequently, if one has unlimited time, and the patience to look through the fat portfolios, or to assort the motley piles of well-thumbed *gravures,* the search proves well worth while. Indeed, these riverside stalls are the paradise of the Grangerite.

The buildings on the opposite side of the street, for the entire length of the quais, are numerously tenanted by antique dealers of every degree. Many of the best antique shops of the city are in this neighborhood. In Paris, the dealers seem to specialize much more than they do in London. One shop will have only oriental objects to offer,—jade earrings, Buddhas, screens, Chinese pottery, etc. Next door one may find nothing but Louis XV furniture, whereas a few shops further, Seventeenth and Eighteenth Century paintings are the exclusive offerings.

In the streets running southward from the river, such as the Rue du Bac, the Rue des Saints Pères, the Rue Bonaparte, the Rue de Seine and the Rue Guénégaud, the lesser antique shops abound. The Rue des Saints Pères is perhaps the most thickly strewn with such inviting dens,—for they are dens, dark, narrow, crowded little *boutiques* where bits of glass and china, and other fragile objects, are so perilously placed that one must step with exceeding care to avoid catastrophe. It has always seemed to me that this plan of display was a considered scheme, a trap for fat ladies and stout gentlemen, who are invariably called upon to pay for any breakage due to careless corpulence or swinging garments. I have witnessed such disasters,—*quorum*, fortunately, *non pars fui*.

One may zigzag through this part of Paris with the certainty of entertainment, and depending upon one's taste, perhaps with profit; for all the intersecting streets of the neighborhood,—the Rue de l'Université, Rue Jacob, Rue de Lille, and others,— harbor dozens of such shops as the antiquer is looking for. And, beyond, are the two great arteries of the Quarter,—the Boulevard St. Germain and the Boulevard Raspail,—with many more such shops, modest and elaborate; and in the little streets that crisscross these avenues there are still more. In the Rue de Rennes, one must stagger from sidewalk to sidewalk to view them all. And so one comes to the Church and the Place of St. Sulpice which is fairly surrounded by antique shops, in the byways that converge there. Here, indeed, is the very birthplace and cradle of the antique business of Paris, and every year in May, in this Place St. Sulpice and the neighboring streets, is held the Foire de St. Germain, which today is the antique dealers' fair. It was anything but such when it began in 1484; but its vicious, riotous and profligate career through the centuries may perhaps account, in the way of normal evolution, for its development into what it is today. Twentieth Century methods are not so vulgarly rough as were those of the Seventeenth; but the result, in the main, is possibly the same.

The Foire de St. Germain started off well under the auspices of the Abbot of St. Germain des Prés, and by the beginning of the Sixteenth Century had acquired fame as a market where the luxuries of Europe and the Orient were to be found. As a natural consequence, no doubt, vice followed upon the trail of luxury, and soon every kind of gambling game known to the times was flourishing in gaily colored tents and booths. The fair became a place for debauch, where foregathered every species of crook, cheat and rascal, professional gamblers, and women of ill repute. They drank hard cider, which was the fashionable beverage of the day, flavored with lemon juice, lime and sugar. This was provided by a Portuguese; and his servitors,—the first to act as *garçons de café* in France,—wore little flaps of linen hanging from the neck which, with time, evolved into the long apron of the present-day French waiter.

Now we know the origin of the Paris *garçon de café*. He is an antique too. But it is surprising that he survived; because, toward the middle of the Sixteenth Century, the students from the near-by Latin Quarter "with staves and daggers" made it their sport to visit the fair for the especial purpose of hunting and destroying "pages, lackeys and other servile creatures." Consequently, for a period of six years, the fair was suppressed by the authorities. They no doubt felt the necessity of a closed season for waiters.

Later on, a new element of discord and riot was introduced into the jovial purlieus of St. Sulpice. Comedians, acrobats, musicians, marionette players invaded these festive precincts. The real simon-pure actors of the Hotel de Bourgogne resented this, and took steps to put the ambulant players out of business. Injunctions were unknown, or at any rate ineffective, in those days. Bludgeons, Greek fire and sharp steel were considered more efficacious. The common people and the students, however, sided with the strolling players, and that settled the question; and very nearly settled the fair. But, after

Napoleon III   Empress Eugenie   Napoleon I   Napoleon III   M. Thiers

RULERS OF FRANCE

several years of brawling, the players achieved official recognition, and one of the troupes of singers and comedians who had thus struggled for their rights called themselves the "Opéra-Comique." From these tumultous beginnings developed the famous Paris Opéra Comique of today.

In the Eighteenth Century the fair fell upon evil days. In 1762 its buildings were destroyed by fire. Then came the Revolution, followed by the Napoleonic wars; and for many years thereafter no fair was held. It might have been entirely forgotten, except by bookworms and collectors of Seventeenth Century prints, if a group of enthusiastic Parisians had not conceived the idea, some years ago, of resuscitating the historic institution. It became a matter of community interest and pride to rehabilitate the spring event that, at one time, had made the St. Germain district famous.

It was decided that the fair should be revived as nearly in its Sixteenth Century aspect as possible; that the booths, the *baraques,* and the open air theatre, should duplicate those of three hundred years ago, and that to make it more realistic, the people of the fair should dress in Sixteenth Century costumes. Obviously, shopkeepers in such attire, in a setting of 1650, could not very well offer modern toys, pottery, glassware and other latter-day products for sale. This would be too anachronistic. Therefore, the costumed dealers must have their booths filled with old furniture, old books, old textiles, and rusty weapons that might have seen service in those days when the students were spearing the lackeys.

By a simple process of logic the fair fell naturally into what it actually is—a gathering place for antique dealers of every kind. And so, every year now, in the springtime, the Place St. Sulpice is fenced in and transformed into a mediæval market place. Antique dealers from all over Paris erect booths into crooked little streets, and appear clad as their ancestors were under Henri III. There is an open air theatre where a company of players from the Opéra Comique give performances of old-time plays. The one I witnessed had something to do with Joan of Arc. There is no gambling or rioting, neither is there any sticking of lackeys (which many visiting foreigners may possibly regret). But there is atmosphere, and French good nature, plenty of opportunity to pick up a worth-while bibelot,—and the fair lasts three weeks.

On the right bank of the river, one finds most of the glorified antique shops, those with dimmed lights and soft carpets,—which call themselves galleries. They are mostly located in the Faubourg St. Honoré and the Rue La Boétie, with one or two in the neighborhood of the Place Vendome. In the Rue de Miromesnil, which branches out of the Faubourg St. Honoré, at the Place Beauveau, there are several good places; and the little streets in that section are worth investigating.

196

Many shops will be found in the Rue de Provence and in the Rue de Chateaudun, which parallels it, as well as in those uphill streets which shoot off thence toward Montmartre. Indeed, the entire district between the Rue de Provence and the Boulevard de Clichy, to the north, is a fruitful field for hunting.

In Montmartre, just beyond, there are any number of little holes-in-the-wall where the patient or the very wise may occasionally discover something. But most of those semi-junk shops of Montmartre, like its restaurants and show places, are stage-set for the verdant tourist.

Like London, Paris has its weekly junk market. It is called the Marché aux Puces, or Flea Market, and has been in existence for some seven hundred years. It is situated just outside the old city fortifications, at the Porte Clignancourt, a twenty-minute taxi ride northward from the centre of the city. One may also reach the Porte Clignancourt by the Metro. The market is held every Sunday, and it is best to get there between nine and ten o'clock in the morning.

The Marché aux Puces was originally a rag fair, whence no doubt its name. From the general appearance of the merchants and pedlars who gather there now, there are no doubt just as many fleas as ever; indeed, I was rather startled one morning by seeing a stout swarthy woman slap herself vigorously on the thigh, giving at the same time a good imitation of a Comanche yell, and then calmly proceed to the

197

search for the victim of her resentment, which she apparently captured and destroyed.

At first sight, the market is rather disappointing, as it appears to consist of endless rows of tawdry booths stretching along the outer edge of the sidewalks of a broad ill-paved avenue, which is swarming with children and dogs playing at death with taxicabs, market carts and clanging tramcars. These booths display, for the most part, shoes, overalls, hats, second-hand clothing and crockery. The low tin-roofed buildings that line the avenue are largely tenanted by purveyors of food, whose specialty appears to be fried potatoes, for in front of almost every one of those tawdry eating places, men in cooks' caps that may once have been white, seem to be eternally dipping *pommes frites* out of great cauldrons, from which emanate almost asphyxiating fumes of lard and fried grease.

But, if you push through this busy, noisy, foul-smelling bazaar for a distance of a couple of blocks, you come to a street which forks off to the left, where you immediately notice a difference in the type of merchandise displayed. There are fewer booths, but the sidewalks are littered with rusty hardware, dented copper utensils, empty picture frames, and a general assortment of absolute junk. A block further on, you reach a sort of fenced enclosure,—what was once a vacant lot,—cluttered with wooden shacks and corrugated iron sheds, placed in a semblance of order, constituting a nest of narrow alleys. Here is the real Flea Market. It is a cosmopolitan district, populated by swarthy men and women from most of the central and eastern European countries,—Russians, Rumanians, Czechs, Greeks, Armenians and Jews. French is the language of the trade, but any other semi-oriental dialect is that of general intercourse. Here and there a steaming samovar is tended by some gypsy girl selling tea or coffee; innumerable dogs dispute the remnants of the sandwiches that have been cast aside; and the blaring of asthmatic gramophones drowns the cries of the hawkers in tunes that were popular in America five or ten years ago.

You wander about in a daze until you become accustomed to the noises, the movement and the atmosphere. You stumble over infant children, you slip into mud puddles, you anthemize "After the Ball Is Over." But presently you become accustomed to all this clamor and disorder, and you begin to notice, through the open doorways of the shacks, furniture and tapestries and brocades and silverware in disorderly heaps.

Obviously most of the wares displayed are worthless, torn, stained, dilapidated or in almost unusable condition. On the other hand, out of the general mess, one not infrequently extracts some desirable object. If you know furniture, you can pick up pieces requiring but slight repair to make them serviceable or even valuable. If you are willing to paw over stuffy piles of textiles, you may find pieces of damask or other material to cover chairs or to make into draperies. But you must know, you must be patient; and you must be capable of bargaining. You must realize that occasionally the dealer knows; and that he probably has infinitely more patience than you have. On the other hand he wants to sell,—and you should not be too eager to buy, except at your own considered price.

Of small objects, such as porcelains, glass, clocks, bottles, boxes and what by courtesy may be termed jewelry, there is a great quantity to be seen. Some of this is genuinely old, most of it is modern trash. The majority of it is in ill repair. But, as before, every now and then, it is possible to pick up something interesting.

There is still another section of the Flea Market a short distance beyond. It is a sort of annex, or overflow. It consists of two parallel thoroughfares about five hundred yards long, and is less noisy, less crowded, and in the main less fruitful to the hunter. But it is worth investigating, for it may harbor just that particular oddity which is being sought for.

THE FLEA MARKET, PARIS
(See pages 197-200)

CHAPTER XIV

HERE is probably no object, however small or insignificant, however useless or ugly, one might even say however large or unwieldy, which is not collected by some enthusiast somewhere. Naturally, environment and opportunity have much to do with inspiration. In the South Sea Islands one is more likely to collect sea shells and war clubs than Fifteenth Century aquatints. One gathers what is to be gathered.

Mr. Henry Ford, I understand, collects stage coaches. He is a man of large interests. The late Dr. Albert Figdor of Vienna, on the other hand, collected toothpicks. At his death in 1927 this collection was put up for sale at auction. It contained so many and such valuable toothpicks,—a considerable number of them dating back to the Fifteenth Century and earlier (Mohammed is said to have sponsored the dainty instrument)—that an entire volume was written about the collection. Newspapers both in Europe and America devoted considerable space to the sale. The New York *Times* even considered the subject editorially:

"An auctioneer of talent is needed to sell the Figdor collection of toothpicks. The leather-lunged gentry accustomed to sell the junk amassed by human magpies would not do for such a fine job. One might suppose that such an extraordinary accumulation of

articles would be held a sacred trust, but it is to go
under the hammer like so many precious and freakish
collections.

"Here are toothpicks fit for a king, and no doubt some
of them have been used on royal teeth. Silver, gold,
ivory set with jewels, enamel and every example of
the jeweler's art are represented. If the enthusiasm for
sleeping in a royal bed, sitting in a chair occupied by
the Prince of Wales for fifteen minutes, and bathing
in King George's marble tub on his former yacht ex-
tends to smaller things, the toothpicks should fetch
high prices. But why, except for utility, should one
want a toothpick? A collection of hundreds of them
is a curiosity; but when it is broken up, the solitary
toothpick, no matter how decorated, loses its charm."

The writer of this editorial must have been of a
cynical nature,—one who probably never collected
anything but grouches, or he would hardly have
generalized jeeringly at "the junk amassed by human
magpies." There is much truth, however, in his last
sentence. What he observes might apply to many
other things that are collected, besides toothpicks.
Just as an object separated from a collection loses a
great portion of the charm it may have possessed
when it was a harmonious member of a homoge-
neous group, so does any other object gain in value
and interest when rescued from incongruous surroundings and associated with others of its kind.
Therein lies much of the joy of collecting,—the
bringing together of similar entities, the recruiting
of families and groups, of whatever oddities these
may consist. A lone private soldier, ambling along
the street, is not a very impressive thing to look
upon. Yet a regiment of soldiers on parade consti-
tutes an inspiring spectacle.

But there are even more curious things than stage-coaches or toothpicks that are sought after by collectors. In the wilds of Ecuador, in the valley of Napo, where few white men care to venture, the more vigorous natives collect the heads of their enemies, which, by some curious process known to themselves, they mummify and shrivel to the size of an orange, without disproportion. I know a man who was honored by one of these Ecuadorean chiefs, not only to the extent of being allowed to retain his own head, but, in addition, to gaze upon the Indian's private collection of occipital trophies, neatly arranged along the crossbeam of his grass-thatched hut. My friend bought one head for one hundred pesos, and this head may now be seen in the Museum of Natural History in New York.

In France, I observed that there were two objects which seem to be of quite general and especial interest to collectors there, but the collecting of which I had never noticed or heard of in England or America. These are toy soldiers, and ivory crucifixes.

I had seen one or two small collections of lead or pewter soldiers in German museums, but it was not until I began antiquing in Paris that I learned that the toy soldier is, and has been for a long time, an object of interest to French as well as to German private collectors. He who was the Crown Prince of Germany, until November 1918, is reported to have a large and particularly valuable aggregation of these little lead men. In Paris there was, at the time of my residence there, a very large collection of pewter soldiers, to the number indeed of 260,000 pieces, which the owner was endeavoring to sell,—and at a very high price. The former Crown Prince was interested in their possible acquisition. Perhaps he owns them now.

The possessor of this collection was a lady who had no interest in these Lilliputian legions, other than what she might be able to sell them for. She was a direct descendant, in the fifth generation, of the one who had begun collecting soldiers. The collectors in the four generations preceding her had been men,— youthful men, we may imagine, retaining through-out their lives a boyish enthusiasm in those martial toys that appeal so strongly to all sturdy youth. And so the army had grown during five generations from perhaps a company, or a regiment, to the size of several divisions.

I never saw the collection. My information how-ever comes from a young man who was well acquainted with it, and who was conducting the negotiations for its sale. He told me he had on many occasions taken part in arranging parades and battles of elaborate proportions. He showed me photo-graphs of some of these. He told me that the collec-tion was begun in the late Eighteenth Century, and still retained many of the contemporary figures. It was under Napoleon, however, that the recruiting assumed serious proportions. Full regiments of im-perial troops were added to the array,—bearded

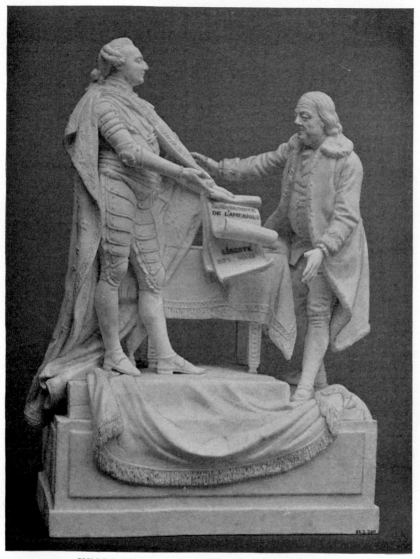

KING LOUIS XVI AND BENJAMIN FRANKLIN

White bisque porcelain group, representing Louis XVI, King of France, and Benjamin
Franklin, Minister from the United States, signing the treaty of Amity and Commerce
between the two nations, February 6, 1778. An exquisitely modelled piece, possibly by
Lemire. Height, 12 inches. Niderviller, c. 1780. There are only seven known examples
of this beautiful bit of ceramic sculpture, of which but one is entirely undamaged.

Huntington Collection, Metropolitan Museum, New York

sappers in long leather aprons carrying great axes, hussars, bashi-bazouks, cuirassiers, the famous Guard. Likewise were represented the enemies of Napoleon,—the Russians, the Austrians, the Spanish, the Italians, the British. The regimental bands were particularly picturesque and colorful.

The Crimean and the Franco-Prussian Wars offered further occasions to add to the variety and number of these cohorts; and apparently he of the generation that saw the World War was an enthusiastic and meticulous collector, for it is alleged that he added a full regiment of every type of soldier in all the contending armies,—including transport, balloon corps, colonial troops, tanks, and great guns!

Even today there are many shops in Paris where a vast selection of lead soldiers may be found. There is one establishment in the Rue des Saints Pères where nothing else is sold. In some of the toy-shops I have seen cavalcades of Napoleon's marshals, all in correct accoutrement and coloring, and with some attempt at portraiture, at least so far as hirsute adornment was concerned,—a noble assemblage on spirited mounts, none over three or four inches high.

There is a sharp contrast between the collecting of these gay toys and the gathering of ivory crucifixes. One must be of morbid mind to wish to indulge in the latter pursuit. A French friend told me that his grandfather collected crucifixes. He had them grouped on the walls of every room in his house. As a boy, my friend was afraid to spend the night at his grandfather's; sleep deserted him surrounded by such gruesome carvings. And yet, in France, there still must be a considerable collectors' interest in ivory crucifixes. There are two shops in Paris, one on the Boulevard Raspail and the other in the Rue des Saints Pères, whose show windows exhibit nothing else.

While these devotional objects may not possess a very general appeal, I am assured that they at least are about the only objects collected in France that are not counterfeited. I doubt if superstition, or even any higher motive of morality, has anything to do with this condition. It is more probable that there is an ample supply to satisfy the existing demand. Not so much may be said of toy soldiers. There is apparently a profitable business in the making of Seventeenth and Eighteenth Century arquebusiers and spearmen.

The story goes that such as these are planted in rural communities, very frequently near a popular inn, or within eye-shot of a crossroads gasoline station. The traveler notices a couple of small boys playing with toy soldiers on an old table under a tree. He approaches and notes eagerly the costume, the clumsy or even crude modeling, and the dulled coloring of the toys. He asks the lads where they got their soldiers, and perhaps, at this juncture, the honest old peasant father or the shrewd grandmother happens along. The traveler learns that no one knows where the toys came from; they had been lying around for years in an old box in the garret. If he is a gullible traveler he purchases the little soldiers, worn and broken as they may be, at a persuasive price that will enable the reluctant little boys to replace them with a very large box of new soldiers in Paris or at the near-by city. And the next day the little boys have still more old soldiers with which to bait the unwary.

The gentle art of faking, in France, and particularly in more southern countries, as Mr. Haraucourt has pointed out, assumes almost the proportions of an industry. In Normandy and Brittany there is a lively trade in "antique" furniture, the making of which, it seems generally conceded, furnishes profitable occupation for many an honest cabinet-maker during the dull winter months. Indeed, in the vacation season, the comic papers of Paris delight in publishing sketches of the sturdy Breton peasant firing birdshot into his bureau or his tall wardrobe, that these may acquire the worm holes so characteristic of genuine old pieces.

At Quimper, in Brittany, famous for its colorful pottery, the factories still produce hundreds of those quaint earthenware figures of the Virgin and the Saints, made from replicas of the old moulds, if not from the old moulds themselves. For perhaps two hundred years or more, these figures had been made for sale to the devout Breton peasants at the Pardons and the fairs. Every home, however humble, has its little pottery figure of the Virgin on the chimney-piece, as well as its crucifix hanging on the wall. In the present generation these figures have been produced in greater quantities, more to supply the tourist demand than to fulfill the wants of the devout peasantry; and as there is a constant demand for "old Quimper," there has developed a considerable business of ageing these modern figures by the various processes well known to the china-faker. Occasionally one finds a genuinely old piece; but it is always damaged and undesirable, else it would long since have been captured by some Paris dealer, many of whom have scoured this countryside for years.

Nevertheless, antiquing in Brittany is more interesting than in any other part of France, chiefly because it is such a picturesque section of the country. Its prehistoric dolmens, its Twelfth Century churches, its quaint roadside crosses, its men with broad beribboned hats and its women with lace headdresses, that vary in every community, make travel there a genuine delight. The roads are excellent, and there are plenty of good inns. I remember particularly the Hotel de France, at Josselin; the Hotel des Voyageurs, at Carnac, where the Druids have left their mark; and the Hotel Julia, at Pont Aven. Here, the Bretons claim, one sees the most beautiful girls in the world,—and their boast has considerable merit. The maids at Pont Aven are certainly the prettiest girls in all of France, with their gay kirtles, flowing ribbons and wonderful lace headdresses. They are blondes for the most part,—quite a dif-

OLD BRASS AND COPPER SHOPS, ST. SERVAN, BRITTANY

ferent race from their inland compatriots,—and their
coifs are the jauntiest in Brittany. Incidentally this
section is a paradise for the collector of laces. The
Breton women, for centuries, have decked themselves
with the finest of *pointe d'Alençon* and *filet Breton,*
—and many exquisite old *fonds de Bonnet* are still
to be picked up.

In St. Malo, which is one of the most interesting
and picturesque cities of Brittany, there are not so
many costumes to be seen, but there is much more of
interest to the antiquer. It is one of the few old
walled towns of France whose ramparts still remain
unimpaired. The streets are winding and narrow,
with here and there little antique shops tucked away
under half-timbered façades, that seem about to
collapse.

In one shop I found a dealer who had a number of
excellent ship models. He was a collector himself,
and after I had overcome his mental and commercial
inertia, he took me up a crooked staircase to a room
above, where he kept those treasures which he called
his own, and that were not for sale. He had some
very fine specimens. He had some good specimens in
his shop, too. I succumbed to a rakish little craft
about six inches long,—a corsair, he called it,—a
charming little miniature with a lacquered or enameled hull, rigging so fine that it may be of horsehair,
and ten tiny brass cannon on the deck, each no more
than a quarter of an inch long.

St. Malo is, or at least has been, a rich field for the

finding of ship models. French prisoners, in the
Napoleonic wars, made quantities of models out of
bone, ivory and wood, during their confinement in
British hulls. Upon their release they sold some of
these before leaving England; but many more models
were brought back to France. St. Malo was one of
the important naval ports of the day, and the men
and their models were dispersed there.

In addition to the models made by prisoners of
war, there are great quantities of *ex-votos,*—offerings hung in the churches, wayside chapels, or even
in their homes, by seafaring men who believe they
escaped calamity or death by making a vow to a
patron saint. A majority of these *ex-votos* are profile
pieces, in frames, many of them of crude workmanship. Others, particularly those that have been hung
in churches, and subsequently removed in exchange
for what the church may need more than ships, are
full-rigged and generally of skilled workmanship.

On the Rue St. Honoré, in Paris, there is a dressmaker's establishment with many *ex-votos,* as well
as ships in bottles, on display in the show window
and along the walls in the interior of the shop. This
seems to be a curious side-line for a dressmaker; but
I believe the explanation is that she spends her sum-
mers in Normandy and gathers ship models and
ex-votos as a profitable pastime. There are several
shops in the Rue Georges, over Montmartre way,
and one in the Rue d'Hauteville, near the Boulevard

Bonne Nouvelle, where ship models are more or less the specialty.

At another little shop in St. Malo, I found a Staffordshire lustre jug. It was one of the first I had seen in France. I have seen many since then. I asked the St. Malo dealer of what make it was. He told me it was of *terre de Jersey*. In Paris one frequently sees Staffordshire lustre jugs in the antique shops. The dealers always tell you they are of *terre de Jersey*.

I had never heard of any potteries on the island of Jersey, and I have since verified the fact that there are none. It seemed curious, therefore, that the French should persist in calling lustre by this name. The explanation, however, seems quite simple. The Channel Islands lie not far off the coast of Brittany. They are geographically much nearer to France than to England. For two centuries or more, between wars, there has been an active trade in fresh foodstuffs between these islands and the ports of northern France. The islanders obtained most of their other necessities and luxuries, such as clothing, furniture and tableware, from England. Staffordshire sent them, among other things, lustre jugs. The French sailors, having nothing similar among the drab potteries of their own provinces, were attracted by the brilliant tones and glazes of these milk jugs which they saw in Jersey, and brought many of them back to their wives and sweethearts. That these jugs were obtained in Jersey was sufficient reason for them to

be considered by the sailor-folk as Jersey jugs,—
hence lustre, in France, is *terre de Jersey*.

This entire northern French coast is dotted with
fishing villages and bathing resorts, with, now and
then, a channel port of greater importance. In every
one of these places there are today one or more antique shops. In most of them the pickings are rather
meagre, and the "antiques" are largely local souvenirs,—cheap chinaware and wretched objects in-
crusted with sea shells. In the larger towns such as
Deauville, Trouville, Honfleur, Havre and beyond,
the offerings are of a greater diversity, with copper
kitchen utensils and broken down wardrobes pre-
dominating. At Honfleur, which is one of the quaint-
est and most picturesque towns of Normandy,—
where painters used to foregather in the days before
charabancs infested and infected the countryside,—
there are two fairly worth-while shops of thoroughly opposite types. One is conducted by a quiet-
spoken English lady, the other by a stout French-
woman of the peasant type. The shop of the latter
is cluttered with great piles of quilts and hangings
(where a patient search will no doubt reward the
hunter), while the outside is draped with bed-
warmers, copper kettles, braziers and old brassware
of every description. The other shop, across the
square, is neatly arranged and contains some attractive china and glassware. I noticed four Sunderland
lustre-rimmed cups and saucers, with pink transfer

GEORGE WASHINGTON

Matchbox of hard paste porcelain, decorated in gold. Height, 5 inches.
Probably of German make, c. 1860. The two lower figures, from
the Metropolitan Museum Collection, are early Nineteenth Century,
the one holding the document inscribed "Patrie" being by Badin
Frères, marked. Height, 8 inches. Both Paris porcelain, c. 1810.

prints of Albert and Victoria. The English lady did not tell me that these were *terre de Jersey*.

At Dives, which is westward of Deauville, there are pottery shops, displaying the most garish and hideous of modern wares, not only of local make, but from other French factories. Sixty or seventy years ago these Dives potteries, which were small concerns, manufactured earthenware and stoneware utensils such as milk jugs, cider jugs, jars and baking dishes, although occasionally they turned their hands to a higher art. In 1851, or thereabouts, they produced figure flasks, somewhat similar to those of Lambeth. Notably, they made a pair of portrait flasks representing Louis Napoleon, and Eugénie. These are of a uniform dark brown color, and of a coarse heavy grade of clay, salt-glazed. The French name for the material is *grès*. The modeling of these pieces is good, but a pair in perfect condition seems rather difficult to find.

The Napoleon flask is thirteen inches high, and shows Louis standing in full uniform and wearing a cocked hat. His right hand is tucked into his buttoned coat, much after the characteristic attitude of his more famous ancestor. Beside him an imperial eagle is perched upon a globe. His left hand rests on an urn inscribed "7,500,000," which was the number of votes alleged to have been cast for him when he was elected president of the Second Republic after the *coup d'état* of 1851. This would seem to indicate that the flask was produced previous to 1852, when Louis proclaimed himself Emperor Napoleon III. The figure of Eugénie is eleven inches high; she holds a prayer book in her left hand clasped to her breast, while a silk purse depends from her right wrist. Her hair is wound about her head in a braid, somewhat like a wreath,—which also points to the date of the piece, for the potter would certainly have decked her with a coronet, had he been modeling a portrait of his empress. Her flaring skirt has three circular flowered flounces, reminiscent of the typical attire of Victoria, as portrayed by the Staffordshire potters.

I have another figure of Napoleon III, similar in attitude to this Normandy flask, and commemorating the same event. It is of porcelain, and is only five inches high. Napoleon stands in full dress uniform, holding his plumed hat in his left hand. His right arm reaches out toward, and the hand almost touches, an urn inscribed in gold script "20 X bre 1851," which was the date of the plebiscite. The figure stands on a square rococo base, and is a graceful bit of statuary. It is intended for use as an ink stand,—the urn to hold the ink. In front of the urn is a small receptacle for a pen. The face, hands, hair and Napoleonic goatee are in the natural colors; all other decoration is in gold. The statuette is of what the French dealers call *vieux Paris*. In the eyes of the majority of French dealers, almost any porcelain figure which is not "Saxe,"—what we call Dresden, —is of *vieux Paris*. A good deal of the *vieux Paris* sold in France nowadays, however, was probably made day before yesterday, and not even in Paris.

There were many small potteries scattered about the outskirts of Paris in the Eighteenth and Nineteenth Centuries, and during the latter period these factories produced a variety of statuettes and figures. Napoleon seems to have inspired them, as he did the Staffordshire potters, and many figures of the little corporal were modeled. The decoration is usually in white and gold, but there are also many decorated in enameled colorings of poor quality, which wear off easily. Figures of various French kings, such as François I and Henri IV were made of *vieux Paris,* but I have never seen any of the Louis. Many busts and figures of these were made at Sèvres.

This Paris porcelain approaches nearer to the sturdy and virile qualities of Staffordshire than any other continental ceramic ware. I have known French dealers, either through ignorance or otherwise, to offer a *vieux Paris* piece as a Staffordshire figure. Staffordshire statuettes of French characters are indeed not uncommon. Aside from Napoleon, the English potters produced many different figures of their neighbors' heroes, particularly at the time of the Crimean War. Probably the same business acumen, which prompted them to manufacture blue and white plates with pictures of American almshouses and other ugly public buildings for export to America, inspired them to make statuettes of Napoleon III and his generals. There is a great variety of Stafford-

215

shire figures, equestrian and others, of Napoleon and Eugénie, of the King and Queen of Sardinia, and of Napoleon and Victoria. General Pélissier, who commanded the French armies in the Crimea, was a favorite subject; and so likewise was Omer Pacha, a Turkish general who fought with the allies against the Russians. Pélissier and Omer Pacha were a choice pair, and have actually become such, ceramically speaking. The former acquired unenviable notoriety in 1845, by putting to death by suffocation some six hundred Arabs who had taken refuge in the caves of Dahra, when France was fighting Algiers. Omer Pacha was not a Turk at all. He was an Austrian officer who absconded with the regimental funds and fled to Bosnia, where he turned Mohammedan and eventually attained high rank in the Sultan's armies. He was dismissed in 1857 for maladministration. Nevertheless, both Pélissier and Omer were heroes, of a sort, especially to the Staffordshire potters, and they make a brave showing modeled in clay on prancing horses, gaily colored in brilliant enamels.

MIRABEAU

CHARLOTTE CORDAY

Typical faience dishes of the period of the French Revolution.
Diameter, 9 inches. Mirabeau was the greatest orator of his
epoch. Charlotte Corday's fame rests upon her assassination
of Marat. The dates on the plates are of their subjects' deaths.

Metropolitan Museum

CHAPTER XV

S we have already had occasion to note,
every collector is constantly finding his
interest aroused in some other form of
art or craftsmanship than that which he
aims consistently to pursue. Yet he would indeed be
a narrow-minded individual who failed occasionally
to succumb to those too frequent temptations. In
fact we should perhaps be grateful to our hobbies for
leading us now and then so pleasantly and profitably
astray. After all, we must have furniture and books,
pictures and clocks, glassware and tea things; a few
brasses, and perhaps even a ship model. Why purchase these in cold blood? Why not acquire them
after a struggle, after a brief resistance to temptation,
or even with a frank plunge into extravagance when
a probably-never-to-occur-again opportunity presents itself? We all have done this thing,—*et haec
olim meminisse juvabit.*

For my own part, I have always found it most
difficult to resist the lure of pottery, in almost any
form. Having a particular weakness for china figures,
it is perhaps not surprising that I have so often
found myself tempted by the charm of dogs, cats,
cows and other animals baked into gay glazes. One
sees many of these in the antique shops of England.
I was there tempted so frequently, and resisted so

frequently, that I finally compromised with my sterner self, and the weaker character of my dual ceramic personality speciously persuaded my resistant individuality with the sordid commercial argument that it might be good business, after all, to assemble a small,—a very small,—collection of animals, which, at some future date, could be sold at a fair profit, which would in turn be used to nourish my particular and principal hobby. Thus it was that I began, from time to time, to acquire little zebras, and lions, and giraffes, and many a breed of dog. This miniature zoo quite fortunately appealed to the distaff side of my household, so that presently it became easier for me to succumb to temptation and even to acquirement by, now and then, bartering for another animal, on the theory that here was a gift rather than an addition to my personal penates.

Indeed dogs, whether natural or of clay, appeal to all men, and I recall again that the first piece of pottery I ever purchased was the majolica mongrel in the market place of Thun. In England, where practically every man owns a dog, it is not surprising that such animal images should find high favor. There are few breeds that were not modeled by the Nineteenth Century Staffordshire potters. The greatest demand appears to have been for spaniels,—with whippets and poodles next in order of popularity.

It is somewhat difficult today to appreciate the enthusiasm which seems to have welcomed the earthenware spaniel in that mid-Victorian period; for in

traveling through England now, it is most unusual
to see even one dog of that breed,—and certainly
none with the gentle, almost inane expression and
stony stare of the conventional mantelpiece ornament. Yet such a vapid dog as that must actually
have existed, else how could so many precise replicas
of its characteristics have been made by so great a
number of different potters? For these china dogs
are always remarkably alike, even to facial expression, with their large ears hanging down on each
side of the face, curiously suggestive of the dear old
ladies of the period, with their pendent curls. Unquestionably, they must be correct representations of
a dog bred very true to type at that time, but belonging to a breed which has been lost, for it corresponds
to no kind of spaniel in England today.

An English china collector investigated this mystery not long ago, and found the solution in some
colored engravings that appeared in an issue of the
Edinburgh Journal of Natural Sciences, published
the year Queen Victoria ascended the throne. Here
he came upon pictures of sixteen different types of
English sporting dogs. He noted that, in nearly
ninety years, the two dogs which had undergone the
least change were the pointer and the setter; but the
rest of the sixteen types had varied greatly, or had
become extinct. There was a picture of a gentle little
dog, sitting humbly in the background, while all the
others were in active sporting attitudes. In every
detail, with its brown ears and brown spots on its

silky coat, its wide open eyes and meek expression, it corresponded precisely to the china dogs of the potteries. It was called the "Comforter."

That the comforter should have completely disappeared, and have left no trace among dogs alive today, may easily be understood when one looks at these pensive little china effigies and sums up the probable merits of the original as a dog.

The china comforters were always made in pairs, —one dog facing the other. They were made in five standard sizes, the largest being eighteen inches and the smallest about six inches in height. The most popular size was nine inches. These solemn creatures vary somewhat in spotting and color design, according to the fancy of the potter, but otherwise they follow a strict formula. The foundation color of the body is white, the ears are of a solid tone, spots of the same color in various shapes and sizes are scattered over the front of the body. The backs are never decorated and only partially modeled. The noses are pink, and the eyes are penciled almost in the form of human eyes, which is possibly what gives these china animals such a pathetic expression. A little gold padlock always hangs from a collar about the neck, and a delicate gold chain falls across the chest and disappears over the back. Red was the favorite color used by the potters in decorating comforters, although there are perhaps just as many of these dogs with gold ears and gold spots. I have seen examples with the coloring in black, brown, green, gray and

M. E. Hewitt

POODLES

Collection of Mrs. Margaret Thorne Smith

D. B. Merrill

A PAIR OF COMFORTERS

Hundreds of these figures were made in Staffordshire during the
mid-Victorian period. (See page 220.)

even copper lustre. I cannot recall ever having seen a blue one, which is odd, as blue was the pigment most successfully and generally used by the potters. I have seen blue cows,—cow creamers decorated with the willow pattern,—but never have I seen a dog so travestied.

The china poodles are usually smaller than the comforters, and are not restricted to the absolutely conventional sitting posture of the latter. The poodles usually hold a little basket in the mouth. They are frequently found in groups of two or three on the same base, and the mane in many cases is put on with dry clay, to give a more natural effect.

There is a great variety, too, among the whippets. We find them sitting, upright and keen, with or without a hare in the mouth; or standing, or lying prone with their paws crossed one over the other. They were favorite models for the decoration of inkstands, the body of the inkstand being usually of a rich dark blue glaze. Some of these whippet pieces are supposed to be representations of actual dogs,—famous racers,—for in mid-Victorian times, even more so than now, and long prior to the day of the electric hare, whippet racing was a great national sport in England, and prize-winning dogs were widely known by name and reputation.

China figures of other breeds of dogs were not made in such great quantities, and for that reason are usually more carefully modeled and colored. Dalmatians, pointers and setters seem to have called for the better skill of the modelers. It is a curious fact that whereas the Staffordshire potters made thousands of dogs, and many groups and pairs of sheep, cows, zebras, lions, gazelles, and other wild and domestic animals,—they modeled very few cats. As a result, earthenware cats are extremely scarce, and become very desirable acquisitions when found.

Nor were horses made to any very great extent, except subordinately as the mounts in equestrian groups, although there are several known statuettes of celebrated race horses, notably the rare early Staffordshire figure of Eclipse. This horse, as all followers of the turf know, and as most of the rest of us probably do not know, is ranked as the greatest race horse of all time. He was foaled during the great eclipse of 1764, from which he derived his name. He was bred by the Duke of Cumberland, who sold him as a colt to an Irish turfman, Dennis O'Kelly. Eclipse ran and won his first race in 1769. He ran in many races during the one year and five months of his brief career, and never was beaten. He won over £25,000 in money prizes for O'Kelly,—a greater sum than had ever been won by any horse,—and plate that is said to have aggregated several tons in weight. At the stud he got 335 winners, whose total winnings amounted to over £160,000. Eclipse died in 1789. "At his interment, ale and cake were given."

Figures of bears are likewise unusual. In the latter part of the Eighteenth Century, when bear-baiting was one of the national sports of England, the potters made quite a number and variety of bear jugs; but after bear-baiting was suppressed, the unfortunate animal seems to have lost favor, and I know of no Nineteenth Century clay tributes to his memory.

Many of my portraits in pottery may more correctly be described as portraits *on* pottery, for they are on jugs,—either modeled in low relief or transfer printed. While portrait-jugs exist in considerable variety, other decorated jugs exist in almost innumerable designs, shapes and sizes. That a jug is a useful object, as well as one of the most primitive forms of the potter's product, no doubt explains why so many of these simple vessels have been made. Every family,—in civilization at least,—possesses one or more jugs. These have a recognized position in the household. How, then, can an antiquer,—whatever his determination may be,—avoid acquiring an additional jug or two, whether he needs one or not? There is something cheery and comforting about the rotund form, the open lip, the convivial suggestion, the inviting handle of a jug. Especially is this so with respect to Sunderland jugs. These are so fat, capacious and squatty; so thoroughly British in their solidity of appearance, in their perfect adherence to tradition, by their unwavering devotion to the bridge over the River Wear.

It was, and perhaps still is, the general practice among the Staffordshire potters to produce the same design of jug in three different sizes, the largest holding about two quarts, the next one quart, and the smallest holding a pint. This is a relic of a condition or custom that prevailed as far back as the reign of King James I, when ale jugs or ale pots were made in four sizes. The gallonier, so-called, held one gallon; the pottle pot held half a gallon, or two quarts; the pot, one quart, and the "little pot" held a pint. Many jug collectors endeavor to obtain all three sizes of the same model, particularly with the sporting and hound-handled jugs of Rockingham, and the stoneware jugs with scenes in relief (the Ivanhoe, Tristram Shandy, Uncle Tom jugs, etc.), made by Ridgways in the 1830's.

In Sunderland, however, the potters were not satisfied with three sizes of jugs. They made sets of six and of twelve,—the largest capable of holding two and three gallons, while the smallest, in a set of a dozen, would be suitable for use as a small cream jug. Full sets of twelve Sunderland jugs in the different sizes are rare. The big fellows are very impressive, extremely decorative, and are almost always brilliantly decorated in lustre, framing transfer prints either of a ship, or of sentimental verses, or of a guild's arms on one side, and the inevitable Iron Bridge over the River Wear on the other.

This bridge seems to have exerted a great fascination over the Sunderland potters, as fully nine out of ten of the jugs, mugs, bowls, basins and other pieces produced there, over a period of nearly one hundred years, are decorated with a picture of this structure. Ceramically, it is the most extensively pic-

ECLIPSE

The Eighteenth Century race horse that never lost a race.
(See page 222.) Staffordshire, c. 1770.

Collection of Miss Edith Feilden

M. E. Hewitt

A PAIR OF WHIPPETS

Mid-Victorian Staffordshire figures.

Collection of Mrs. Margaret Thorne Smith

tured bridge in the world. Finished in 1796, it was considered a great engineering achievement for those times, and the potters proclaimed the wonder for nearly a century. There are collectors whose acquisitive desires are restricted to Sunderland pottery decorated with a picture of this now famous Iron Bridge. It is usually depicted from the west, but there are also views taken from the east. Some of these views show a kiln on the shore to the right; in other views there is no kiln,—or it has been moved over to the left. Sometimes there is a horse-drawn vehicle crossing the bridge; sometimes not. The design of the great span varies in the transfers of different potters, —some have it flat, some have it high in the centre. Indeed, here is a fertile field for the specialist.

But the principal charm of Sunderland ware is its lustre, particularly its pink and its mottled lustre. Curiously enough, the fakers have not yet turned their attention to the counterfeiting of the latter, or else they have not succeeded in discovering any method that is commercially profitable. Mottled lustre, which is typical of Sunderland and seldom if ever found on other wares, is mostly seen in the decoration of mugs, jugs, bowls and placques, whereas the simpler pink or purple lustres are more often found on tea sets and table ware. I have seen a few, but only a very few, figures or animals decorated in mottled lustre. This peculiar effect is due to the bursting of oil bubbles in the glaze mixture when it is first subjected to the heat of the kiln.

225

The Sunderland potters were not gifted with much imagination,—as may be inferred from their hundred-year adherence to the bridge motif. Thus, Sunderland table ware or tea sets, while for the most part charming in form and color, have but little variety of decoration. There are practically only two Sunderland designs, and these might be called standard, although, being done by hand, no two decorations are ever exactly alike, even in a definitely related set. One decoration is known as the "Cottage" design, and pictures a house or a barn of the rural English type, with occasionally a tree or a fence to fill in. The other design is known as the "Primitive," and consists of crude drawings, in outline, of houses with flat roofs and cock-eyed chimneys, such as we used to create with our little paint brushes at about the age of three. Nevertheless, these are quaint and delightful, and particularly well adapted to lustre. I have never seen this Primitive design in any other color.

The Staffordshire lustre jugs,—which are copper lustre,—are more solid in appearance, and usually decorated with brightly colored bands or raised floral motifs, or both. Occasionally one finds a lustre jug with a medallion portrait, and sometimes with a more elaborate pictured scene of some historic event, such as the surrender of Cornwallis at Yorktown. Unfortunately, the faker has been busy counterfeiting Staffordshire lustre, but there are, nevertheless, still frequent opportunities to obtain genuine pieces.

The imitations, mostly made in Germany or Czechoslovakia, are usually rather heavy and thick, and the lustre is likely to be dull.

It is a curious fact that in the Paris antique shops one sees many lustre jugs, always designated by the dealers as being of *terre de Jersey*. A fair proportion of these seem to be genuine Staffordshire, gathered no doubt among the little seaports along the channel coast. Many, if not the majority, are of modern Czechoslovakian manufacture, some being excellent imitations, although usually lacking in the softness and brilliancy of the real article.

The old silver lustre has not been very successfully imitated in modern times, and attempts to reproduce silver lustre commercially have failed. In the beginning silver lustre tea sets were made to copy the forms of Georgian silverware, in an endeavor to provide, at a lower price, something that might take the place of silverware. But this experiment was apparently not very successful. Silver lustre cost more to the purchaser than the ordinary decorated tea set, and was just as fragile. It is rather unusual today to find complete sets of genuine old silver lustre tea or coffee services. There is a good collection of such pieces in the museum at Stoke.

A favorite way of using lustre, particularly copper and pink mottled lustre, was in the coloring of the frames of earthenware placques. Many such placques were made in Staffordshire and in Sunderland. They are rectangular and usually about eight by ten or twelve inches in size, and bear transfer prints of individuals, religious mottoes, ships, and occasionally manor houses or rural scenes. Pictures of early railroad trains are rare and extremely desirable. The frames of these placques are more or less elaborately modeled in imitation of the heavily gilded rococo frames used on the paintings of the period. Staffordshire placques frequently have no lustre decoration, but the frames of Sunderland placques are invariably brilliant with pink or mottled lustre, and the pictures, of course, are very frequently of the famous Wear bridge. There are always two holes near the top centre of these placques,—sometimes in the frame itself, sometimes just below it,—for the insertion of the string with which to hang the picture on the nail in the cottage wall.

One day, at the Caledonian Market, among a mass of crockery spread out over the cobbles, I espied a brightly framed placque, bearing a transfer-printed picture of a full rigged ship. I picked it up and examined it carefully. There was not a nick or a crack in it, and the purple mottling bubbled gaily in what little sunlight there was. I turned it over and saw that it bore an impressed underglaze mark "Dixon Co."

Now I knew perfectly well that Dixon was one of the best known names among the Sunderland potters; but my recollection was that the firm name was Dixon & Company, or Dixon & Dixon, and I seemed to remember that the impression of these

H. H. Costain

A COLLECTION OF PORTRAIT JUGS

names was usually, if not always, in capital letters. I felt rather suspicious of the mark on the placque that I held in my hand,—but it was a very interesting placque. The barrowman shambled up to me and assured me that here was a fine piece of genuine Sunderland ware. His price, however, seemed to me entirely too reasonable, even in the Caledonian;—it was but a few shillings. I queried the typography of the mark, but the dealer was apparently unfamiliar with such trifling details. He insisted that any piece marked "Dixon" was obviously genuine Sunderland. There seemed to be no advantage in arguing this question with him, although I think I did point out meekly and tactfully that marks might sometimes be faked. However, I finally bought the placque with the mental reservation that, even if it was a fake, it was extremely decorative,— and, after all, one must take chances at the Caledonian Market, if one is not an expert on marks. I decided not to let indecision rob me of a possible prize.

When I got home, I looked into my book on pottery marks and found there listed the following Sunderland indications: "DIXON, AUSTIN & CO.," "DIXON & CO. SUNDERLAND," "W. DIXON," "DIXON & CO.,"—but no "Dixon Co." I concluded that I had been rash. However, I consoled myself with the thought that every collector must occasionally make a mistake, and after all it was a very charming placque, and the faker had done a good job.

A few days later, I wrapped up my purchase and took it to my friend, the dealer in Great Turnstile. I told him I had bought something at the Caledonian Market, and that I thought it was a fake. He smiled indulgently, and with an expression of friendly commiseration for anyone who would buy anything at the Caledonian. I unwrapped my placque and handed it to him, explaining that I had suspected the mark, but that I liked the piece, and had been willing to take a chance. He fondled it in both hands, looking meanwhile dreamily at the ceiling.

"It *feels* right," he said presently; "I believe it *is* right. But I never saw this mark before."

"Faked?" I suggested, briefly.

"Pretty dangerous business, faking marks," he replied. "It feels right to me. Let's look it up in Chaffers."

He went to the back shop and returned with his Chaffers, which was a volume about the size of two or three encyclopedias rolled into one. He looked up "Dixon," and ran his finger down the columns, shaking his head as he read. Finally he paused at a paragraph in small type.

"Here it is," he exclaimed, " 'Dixon Co.,' a small factory that only worked a short time! You did not get let down after all," and he seemed genuinely delighted. "It felt right to me," he repeated.

I then learned from him that, from long practice, he felt confident that even with his eyes closed he could tell, by the feel of any pottery, of just what make it was. I determined to try him out some day; and a few weeks later the opportunity arose. I had bought a sugar bowl in a little shop in Putney. The dealer had said it was Bow, because it had a "B" scratched on the bottom, underglaze. I felt confident that it was not Bow, but it was well worth the few shillings it was priced at, and I bought it to give to a friend who collects tea sets. It was gracefully shaped, and gaily decorated with little sprays of flowers. I took it soon afterward to Great Turnstile and told my friend the dealer I had a marked piece that I wanted him to identify with his eyes closed. He consented willingly, and I handed him the parcel. He closed his eyes, unwrapped the bowl and ran his hands over it several times. Then he handed it back to me saying:

"That's Flight & Barr Worcester,"—and it was, as he conclusively proved to me in other ways.

I have known several collectors who had this gift of being able to identify china by the touch, but no one who had it to such great refinement as the late Sir William Van Horne, who, as a diversion from building and managing Canadian railroads, collected Japanese ceremonial teacups. He was showing me his collection one day at his home in Montreal, and detailing the fine points that marked the value and rarity of his exquisite specimens. I was wholly ignorant of the lore of Japanese ceremonial teacups,— and still am,—but Sir William explained that collectors of these precious pieces set great store upon

231

those made by certain artisans. These Seventeenth and Eighteenth Century Japanese potters were indeed artists, and some of these delicate cups made by the more noted are of great rarity and are estimated accordingly. Sir William told me that he had so schooled himself in the fine points of his hobby that, with his eyes closed, he could not only tell the make of any cup but also the name of the potter who had thrown it.

I suppose my doubt was ill-veiled by the frankness of my astonishment, for he proceeded to assure me that not many months before, while he was in Washington, he had been invited by the then Japanese Ambassador to look upon some priceless ceremonial teacups in the latter's collection. Sir William, at a glance, had named some of these cups, and upon the expression of the diplomat's surprise, he had said to him, what he had just said to me, that he could identify by the potter's name any cup in the collection. The Japanese gentleman, being confidently incredulous that any man, particularly an occidental, could possess such skill, promptly said that he had two unique cups in his cabinet with which he would like to test Sir William's ability, and that if Sir William could do as he said he would *give* him the cups. I do not remember, at this late date, if this test took on the nature of a wager, and if Sir William was to forfeit anything if he failed, but I do know that Sir William turned his back to the ambassador and accepted one cup after the other, holding his hands behind him, and named the potters of both pieces.

Cups,—not Japanese ceremonial teacups,—but the ordinary tea or coffee cups of homely English life, also tempted me on many occasions during my antiquing adventures in Europe. Half a century ago tea sets were made with two kinds of cups, those of the conventional shape of the present day, which had saucers, the others being shaped like shaving mugs, although smaller. And they were called mugs. The boys of the family had their tea out of the mugs, and the girls were served in the cups. Odd, or individual, mugs were also made, in all kinds of ware from the finest Worcester and Chelsea porcelain to the commonest of earthenware. Many of these mugs are decorated with mottoes, verses, and pictures, or labeled with names, as "For John," "For Mary," "For a good boy," and frequently with such local inscriptions as "A trifle from Lowestoft." I have seen several collections of mugs and they make a brave showing. Even a few well selected specimens add greatly to the charm and variety of a china cabinet. To the specialist they offer an attractive field. One may gather the Alphabet, or Ben Franklin's Maxims, or Æsop's Fables, and even various aspects of the Iron Bridge across the Wear. Curiously enough, there are not many such mugs bearing portraits of notables. The potters seem to have considered that portraiture deserved the greater importance, perhaps the more elaborate display, of the rotund side of a jug, or the framed panel of a teapot.

Many portraits are to be found on teapots. One of the earliest is the salt-glazed piece, in the Willett Collection, made in 1740 to commemorate Vernon's victory at Porto Bello, and decorated with a medallion portrait of the Admiral. Castleford teapots were often decorated with portraits in low relief. This delicate ware was made only between 1790 and 1820, a period during which the English potters were particularly catering to the American market. Thus, we find Castleford teapots with portraits of Washington, Franklin, the capped head of Liberty, and the arms and eagle of the United States.

At about the same period, that is between 1790 and 1815, Felix Pratt was producing a distinct type of ware at Lane Delph, in Staffordshire. His work may easily be identified by the lightness of its weight, the peculiar blue tinge of its glaze, the individual style of modeling, and the fine quality of the coloring. Pratt's ware is the only Staffordshire product that bears any affinity to that of the great Italian majolicists; his color palette has the same simple restriction to cobalt blue, a soft green, a rich orange and a warm brown. Pratt's teapots were formed much after the long-shaped fashion of Castleford, either oval, flattened oval, or irregular. He made no round teapots. The tops of the lids were usually modeled in the form of a swan, or a dolphin, or a seated figure.

Pratt made a number of portrait-teapots, and a considerable variety of portrait-jugs,—but he was

ADMIRAL, LORD RODNEY

Earthenware mug. Height, 6 inches. Staffordshire, 1780.

Willett Collection

H. H. Costain

DUKE OF WELLINGTON

Stoneware jug with embossed figures, richly enameled and glazed. Height, 4¾ inches. Staffordshire, c. 1814.

more of a British patriot than most Staffordshire potters, and modeled his own national heroes. He had a fixed method of portraying admirals and generals. The admirals appear emerging from the sea, which is suggested by a green wavy surface decorated with one or two fishes' heads. The generals are mounted on the conventional prancing chargers. The name of the personage portrayed is usually inscribed on a scroll. On one of Pratt's earliest jugs are two generals riding across country. They represent, and are labeled, the "Duke of York," son of George III, and "Prince Cobourg." These two princes were in command of their respective forces in the Netherlands campaign of 1794. After the naval victories off Camperdown and St. Vincent in 1797, Pratt made jugs with the portraits of Admiral Duncan and Captain Trollope. He also made a Lord Jervis jug, and jugs celebrating Nelson's victories at the Nile and at Trafalgar. The Nile jug bears a portrait of Nelson on one side and of Captain Berry, his flag captain, on the other.

CHAPTER XVI

N the minds of many collectors, there is a considerable misapprehension as to the precise designations for the periods in which the quality of Staffordshire, and indeed of almost all other English pottery, so greatly varied. The terms "old Staffordshire," "early Staffordshire," "early Nineteenth Century," and "early Victorian" are confusingly and indiscriminately employed. This is all the more surprising, as the chronology is quite simple, and easy to understand.

Auction catalogues are the principal offenders in misguiding, and misinforming. In most of them the terms "early Staffordshire" and "old Staffordshire" are applied to almost every listed piece of this ware, regardless of age or quality. Collectors, too, often seem to consider "early Nineteenth Century" and "early Victorian" as synonymous terms, whereas a moment's reflection will make it obvious that the early Victorian period can in no sense be considered as early Nineteenth Century. Victoria's reign did not begin until 1837, when one-third of the years of the Nineteenth Century had already elapsed. She reigned during all the remaining years of that century, which is thus dynastically divided into two proportionate parts,—or as one-third is to two-thirds.

The greater portion of the early years of the Nineteenth Century are included within the reign of George III. Most of us are inclined to associate this monarch with hose and periwig, with the Declaration of Independence and the days of Bunker Hill. But George III had a very long reign. If he had lasted a few years longer he would have come to wear long trousers. His successor, George IV, did. He was the first English King to get into long pants. He ruled from 1820 to 1830. William IV occupied the throne from 1830 to 1837. Thus these three kings reigned during the first third of the Nineteenth Century, a period which is now, ceramically at least, usually designated as the early Nineteenth Century period.

Victoria's reign extended over the last two-thirds of the century, and is not only ceramically, but in a certain measure, historically divided into three distinctive periods,—the early Victorian, from her accession to 1860; the mid-Victorian, from 1860 to 1880; the late Victorian, from 1880 until her death in 1901. These epochs fall rather naturally into twenty-year divisions,—periods which happen to have been accentuated by certain outstanding political and social conditions, not only in England but in Europe generally. There is, however, no sharp line of demarcation between them; each one flowed gradually into the other.

During the first period, Albert was Prince Consort. During the next twenty years the world was considerably unsettled by wars and political upheavals.

The results of the Indian Mutiny were still being felt in England, (figures of Napier, Dundas, and others were made by the potters); the Prince Consort died in 1862, placing Victoria and all England in mourning; our own Civil War lasted from 1861 to 1865, (the potters made figures of John Brown, Uncle Tom, Lincoln, etc.); the Franco-Prussian War and the fall of the Second Empire occurred in 1870, (figures of Napoleon III were produced in quantities); the Russo-Turkish War lasted from 1877 to 1878 and the Zulu War was fought in 1879.

The last twenty years of Victoria's reign covered a period of general world peace (with the exception, for England, of the Boer Wars), but it was a dull and, intellectually, a somewhat dreary era.

Ceramically, the most important periods in England were the latter half of the Eighteenth Century and the first quarter of the Nineteenth,—the years in which Josiah Wedgwood and Enoch Wood were doing their best work and strongly influencing the efforts and endeavors of all other English potters. Both of these great leaders were Staffordshire men. The pottery products of Staffordshire were, in their time, by far the most important in England. This does not mean that other sections were not producing wares of high merit, for Worcester, Chelsea, Derby, Bow, Liverpool, Bristol and Leeds were then likewise at their zenith. But the latter were, in a sense, specialists, whereas the Staffordshire men attempted all things and succeeded famously in most,

—with the exception of the delicate porcelains. Commercially they surpassed all the others. Their output was enormous. Their export trade, for those times, was world wide. It was a British envoy to Russia, I think, who declared that on his long voyage from London to Moscow, his dinner was served, at every inn and hostel, upon Wedgwood dishes.

But our theme is not of ceramics in general. It is rather of that limited, perhaps inconsequential collateral development of the industry which furnished a vehicle for the art of the sculptor, and resulted in those dainty and vigorous as well as commonplace figures and statuettes which have captivated our present interest.

While it is true that figures were made at Chelsea, Leeds, Plymouth, Rockingham and many other factories, so many more, and in such great variety, were produced in Staffordshire, that collections of figure pieces, unless specialized, always include a vast majority of examples from the Five Towns, and the casual collector is likely to think of china figures, in general, in terms of Staffordshire. Even Rockingham figures, which were made in considerable variety, and average higher in merit than Staffordshire cottage ware, are frequently misrepresented by ignorant dealers as Staffordshire, and are accepted as such by those who seem to be unable to distinguish between porcelain and earthenware.

The present chronological observations, therefore, while applying in particular to Staffordshire figures, may be applied pretty generally to the plastic products of all the English factories.

The period in which the finest pieces were produced was during the last quarter of the Eighteenth Century. The term "old Staffordshire" is applied by common practice and general acceptance to the products of those years. As we have already agreed, there is no sharp dividing line, no exact year or date, separating any one ceramic period from another.

The products of the first twenty-five or thirty years of the Nineteenth Century—extending even to the time of Victoria's accession in 1837, are generally referred to as "early Nineteenth Century Staffordshire," usually abbreviated to "early Staffordshire." Here, unfortunately, is a frequent source of misunderstanding and confusion; for the abbreviation to "early Staffordshire," by the very sense of the words, implies reference to the period conventionally designated as "old Staffordshire" and applies to the products of the middle years of the reign of George III. "Early Staffordshire"—more specifically "early Nineteenth Century Staffordshire"—was produced in the latter part of his reign, and under George IV and William IV. The Victorian periods followed. There were no great potters in the Victorian age, although Enoch Wood lived for five years after Victoria became queen. But he was then a very old man, and none of his work may properly be included with that of the Victorians.

240

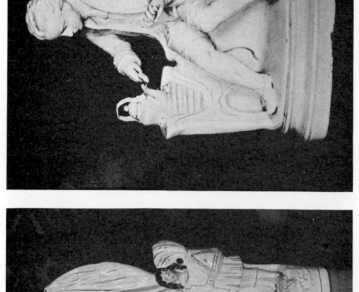

KING JOHN SIGNING MAGNA CHARTA

White and gold group. Height. 13 inches.
Staffordshire, c. 1820. (See page 97.)

JAMES WATT

Delicate bisque porcelain statuette of the discoverer of
the power of steam. Castleford. c. 1810.

A glance at the chart on page 242 will give a clear idea of the relationship and inter-relationship of these periods, and will help to convey to the reader at once a visual appreciation of the dates within or after which certain portrait pieces were or could have been produced, and, more important yet, will indicate clearly the dates at which such portrait pieces could not have been produced.

In the early years of the mid-Victorian period white and gold figures became popular, and were made in considerable variety of subject by the Staffordshire potters. They are designated as white and gold pieces, because, unlike the earlier highly colored statuettes, these bear no other decoration than a slight gold penciling, except on the hands, heads and boots, which are usually decorated in the natural colors. In equestrian figures the horse's mane is penciled in gold, the reins and trappings are piped in gold, and the animal is usually dappled with gold spots, arabesques, or small geometric designs, the like of which no self-respecting horse ever displayed.

It was at about this time, too, that the potters adopted the manner of labeling or identifying their figures by inscribing the name of the character, in raised letters, across the base of the piece. This style of labeling serves as an excellent, although not infallible, method of determining the period of manufacture of many of these Nineteenth Century figures and groups.

In the latter part of the Eighteenth Century when

CHRONOLOGICAL TABLE OF ENGLISH
CERAMIC PRODUCING PERIODS

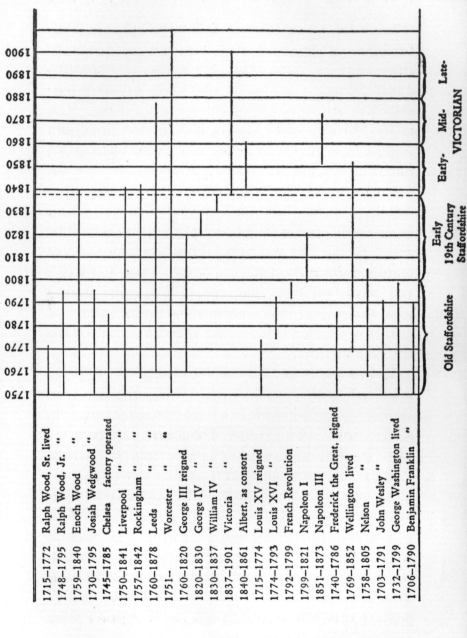

1715–1772	Ralph Wood, Sr. lived
1748–1795	Ralph Wood, Jr. "
1759–1840	Enoch Wood "
1730–1795	Josiah Wedgwood "
1745–1785	Chelsea factory operated
1750–1841	Liverpool " "
1757–1842	Rockingham " "
1760–1878	Leeds " "
1751–	Worcester " "
1760–1820	George III reigned
1820–1830	George IV "
1830–1837	William IV "
1837–1901	Victoria "
1840–1861	Albert, as consort
1715–1774	Louis XV reigned
1774–1793	Louis XVI "
1792–1799	French Revolution
1799–1821	Napoleon I
1851–1873	Napoleon III
1740–1786	Frederick the Great, reigned
1769–1852	Wellington lived
1758–1805	Nelson "
1703–1791	John Wesley "
1732–1799	George Washington lived
1706–1790	Benjamin Franklin "

242

Wedgwood, Wood, Pratt and other talented Staffordshire artists were modeling figures and busts, their subjects were either mythological,—Jupiter, Juno, Neptune, etc.,—or characters of such outstanding historical importance,—as the King, Voltaire, Milton,—that titular inscriptions no doubt seemed superfluous. Of course, some pieces bore titles, but this was not the general practice. Later, in the first quarter of the Nineteenth Century and after, figures were made in much greater numbers, of far lesser merit, and with an appeal to a much broader and less cultured audience. This less sophisticated market apparently needed to be told what was what, and who was who, and consequently the potters took to labeling their figures and groups. This was not an invariable practice, but it became more or less the general rule.

It was approximately under George IV that the practice became prevalent, and the inscriptions were almost uniformly made in a bold flowing script, usually in gold. The "Death of Nelson" group facing page 74 affords an example of this style of lettering.

Early in the reign of Victoria, a new style was quite generally adopted, and the inscriptions were made in low relief block letters, the raised faces of which were usually decorated in gold. These letters were somewhat fancy, being adapted from a typeface devised by the early lithographers, who were then just developing their new art. Among typographers this face is designated as "Egyptian with split serifs,"—for what reason "Egyptian" I have never been able to find out. It is a type-face which apparently appeals to the multitude, for it soon spread to France where it achieved great popularity, and where it is still widely used. The awnings of almost every Brasserie and Café and Tobacconist in France are inscribed in this style of lettering, even until this day. The inscription on the base of the figure of Lincoln, facing page 84, is an example of this style.

The bold script form of inscription on Staffordshire figures and groups was used, roughly speaking, from the middle of the early Nineteenth Century period through the early Victorian period, that is to say from about 1820 to 1860. The Egyptian style of lettering was general during the mid-Victorian period, that is from 1860 to 1880. From then on, as the art of potting degenerated, crude and clumsy variations of the block type were used; frequently relief lettering was discarded, and if the potter placed any inscription whatever on his wares, he did this quite carelessly with a brush, in an attempted imitation of block lettering. Most of the later copies and reproductions of early Victorian figures and groups bear these crude scrawls instead of modeled or relief letters.

It should not be understood that there was any distinct or precise cleavage in the periods of the use of these styles of lettering. The periods overlapped, or flowed gradually from one into the other, but, in general, the date of manufacture of any piece bearing either of these types of inscription may be pretty safely assumed to be within the decades indicated above. An inscription in bold gilt script on any piece is pretty good evidence that it was produced prior to 1860, although I have seen several pieces with script titles the dates of which could be otherwise definitely determined as of 1861. A piece titled with carefully modeled Egyptian lettering was almost certainly produced between 1860 and 1880. Dull and careless lettering is characteristic of the later years of the Nineteenth Century.

It was about 1870, or shortly thereafter, that a decadence of the potter's art became noticeable. As we have mentioned previously, methods of transportation had greatly improved by that time, and quantity production soon followed. Not quantity production in our Twentieth Century sense of the word,—but production in far greater quantity than the demands of the trade had hitherto warranted. The result was that the mass of Staffordshire potters, who always had been a lot of copyists and pirates, proceeded to imitate the best work of their more competent predecessors, to make moulds from pieces that they were unable themselves to equal in quality of workmanship, and to turn out reproductions which are now all too frequently confounded with the genuine product of an earlier day. In addition, be it said in their favor, they made a great variety of original pieces,—cottage ornaments and similar models,—which, although inferior artistically to the work of the earlier potters, nevertheless possessed a certain virility, quaintness and even individuality, which are justly recognized today.

We must not confuse these early reproductions, or pirated copies of other artists' successful models, with the deliberate fakes and forgeries of a later date. The early Victorian potters imitated the work of their contemporaries and of their immediate predecessors, just as one dressmaker copies another dressmaker's "creation" today. They seized upon designs and technical processes wherever they found them, and offered these counterfeit wares for sale as original products of their own. They profited on other men's ideas, but they did not trade on other men's names.

The forgeries of modern times have been perpetrated from entirely different motives. These recent imitations have been put forth as the work of noted potters, and thus the fakers have tried to trade upon name and fame as much as upon the intrinsic merit of the objects they have plagiarized.

There is a firm in London which has been in the pottery business for over one hundred years. It is a highly reputable concern, but it deals quite extensively in reproductions of Staffordshire cottage pieces, which are sold at very cheap prices, and frankly as reproductions. This is all very well so far. The fact remains, however, that these reproductions are bought in considerable quantities by unscrupulous dealers in England and America, are aged

GEORGE WASHINGTON
White earthenware covered with a clear buff glaze, modeled by Enoch Wood.
Height, 8½ inches. Staffordshire, 1818. (See overleaf.)

Collection of Lord Revelstoke

GEORGE WASHINGTON

Back of bust, pictured on the preceding page, showing panel, inscribed with the
mark of Enoch Wood and the date the piece was produced.

by the processes known to all fakers, and sold to gullible purchasers as old Staffordshire pieces. The manufacturer piously disclaims all responsibility. He argues that he cannot control his customers. On the other hand he makes no effort to protect the public. He places no mark upon his reproductions that would identify them as such. It would be quite easy to impress every piece underglaze with a letter "R," or the word "Reproduction,"—but doubtless this would interfere with a profitable trade.

There is another manufacturer who, for the past forty years or more, has made a specialty of reproducing those objects which are in especial demand by collectors, largely by American collectors. He, too, disclaims any intention to deceive. He offers the specious excuse that many collectors admire quaint and beautiful things, and are quite willing to own reproductions if they cannot obtain originals. But his trade is not with collectors; it is wholesale with dealers. He has, to a certain extent,—and perhaps as a left-handed compliment to the American trade,— specialized in jugs and bowls with transfer printed portraits of Washington and Lafayette (marked "Ricd Hall & Son, 1824"); certain Dr. Syntax plates; statuettes of Benjamin Franklin; and a blue-coated bust of Washington, generally attributed to Enoch Wood.

It would appear that Enoch Wood modeled two different busts of Washington. Perhaps he made several. Of these two pieces, one was produced about

217

1790, and is not marked; the other was made in 1818 and is marked. The earlier bust is almost invariably decorated with a blue coat; forgeries and imitations of it have been made from the time of Wood until today. Perhaps it was because this bust was being so freely pirated, even in his own lifetime, that Enoch Wood modeled the second bust and elaborately marked it, to identify it as his own handiwork, and perhaps as a means of protecting it from the pottery pirates. He apparently also numbered every copy with an impressed serial number.

The portraiture of the 1818 bust is of Washington in his declining years, the face being more serious and more idealistic than that of the earlier piece, which pictures him more as he must have looked in the prime of life. It also has certain minor characteristics of detail that do not appear in the earlier bust; for instance, the blue busts have either a white or a black jabot, whereas the 1818 model shows Washington wearing an elaborate lace-frilled shirt front. The 1818 bust does not show the mole on the right cheek.

While a considerable number of the blue-coated bust were doubtless produced in the closing years of the Eighteenth Century, it has since become a favorite subject for forgery. Spurious copies are frequently met with in English and American antique shops, and many of these have no doubt found their way into private collections. It is so easy to identify these modern reproductions as frauds that it is somewhat difficult to understand how dealers, whether dishonest or ignorant, can obtain for them the high prices which unwary or inexperienced purchasers seem willing to pay. There is one simple method of identifying most of these modern fakes. On the originals, that is, those made in Enoch Wood's time and possibly produced by Wood himself, Washington's waistcoat displays only two buttons below the jabot, and these are carefully modeled, as well as colored. In the later imitations there are three, four, sometimes five buttons, put on with the brush like the rest of the waistcoat decoration; but a careful scrutiny will disclose traces of the modeled buttons under the enameling. Furthermore, the fancy design on the waistcoat is not the same on the copies as on the early pieces. The jabot on copies is black. On the originals the jabot is usually white, although many genuine pieces are known with black jabots. The spurious busts are made of a coarser clay and weigh not less than one pound and a half, sometimes slightly more. The early pieces weigh slightly over one pound. The forgeries are of the same size as the originals, which would seem to indicate that they were made from a clay model copied from the original, and not from a mould cast from an original pottery bust. In the latter case the copies would be smaller in size, for the clay shrinks about one-eighth in the firing.

Apparently not many examples of the 1818 bust have survived, and these are treasured in private collections or museums. There is one in Lord Revelstoke's Collection and one in that of Mr. R. T. Halsey, now resting in the American Wing of the Metropolitan Museum, New York. Lord Revelstoke's piece, shown facing pages 246 and 247 is of white earthenware covered with a clear buff glaze and has no decoration in color. Its number is 366. Mr. Halsey's piece, numbered 254, is decorated, having a light green coat, brown waistcoat, the face in the natural colors. The pedestal is black. The mark on the back of both pieces is the same, and reads:

WASHINGTON
BORN 1732
DIED 1799

ENOCH WOOD SCULP.
1818

So far as I know, this bust of Washington has never been forged. There are perhaps so few specimens in existence that the fakers have as yet found no opportunity for reproducing it.

But there are other tricks in the faking trade, aside from potting from old models. While looking about an antique shop in London one day, I noticed a number of plates and dishes rather crudely decorated with ships, and portraits, and historical scenes. I examined one and noted that it bore the impressed underglaze mark of Wedgwood. I scrutinized others and noted some Leeds marks. I could not believe that either the Wedgwood or Leeds factories could ever have turned out such inferior work. The pictures looked as if they had been drawn by the veriest amateur. They were intended to simulate transfer prints, but it was quite obvious that the designs had been done by hand, and it was apparent to the touch that they had been applied overglaze and had not been transfer-printed underglaze.

Among the several pieces there was one square cream ware dish, eight by ten inches in size, and about three inches in depth. It was decorated in black with a picture which I at once recognized as a copy of John Trumbull's painting of the surrender of Cornwallis, which hangs in the Trumbull Gallery in the Museum of Fine Arts at Yale. The base of this dish was plainly impressed with the Wedgwood mark. The dealer assured me with great impressiveness that here was a most interesting piece of genuine Wedgwood, over one hundred years old. Americans are supposed not to be interested in anything that is less than one hundred years old. Foreign dealers seem to think that the possibility of taking home some object free of payment of duty is as important an element in an American's decision to purchase as the artistic value of the object under consideration.

I examined the dish very carefully and noted its excellent condition. Knowing that it is rather dangerous to forge pottery marks in England, I was considerably puzzled. It also seemed strange that the dealer should offer these historic Wedgwood and Leeds pieces at such low prices. The Cornwallis dish was priced at thirty shillings. I felt sure that, had these several objects been genuine pieces, they would

251

have been saleable at from ten to twenty pounds each. I decided to purchase the Cornwallis dish, prompted by the feeling that a photograph of it would make a good illustration for this book, and might, perhaps, serve to warn other collectors against similar frauds. The suave dealer was even willing to guarantee the genuineness of my purchase on the receipt I asked him to give me. He also guaranteed the hundred years. Almost any European dealer will do that. I have often wondered how they obtain so accurate a knowledge of the dates of manufacture of so many different kinds of objects, which they can only have possessed for a very short period of time. Perhaps they have some occult method. At any rate, occult or not, it seems to work wonderfully with nine out of ten purchasers, who accept a dealer's idle word, or "guarantee," as gospel, and place profound faith in an assertion which their commonsense ought to tell them is scarcely within human possibility to make.

As I left his shop, the dealer told me that the dishes I had been examining were in great demand, particularly by Americans, and he showed me half a dozen plates decorated with ships, which he had just sold to the representative of a large New York department store, and which were about to be packed for shipment.

The next day I took my Cornwallis dish to the Wedgwood offices in Hatton Garden and showed it to the manager. He agreed with me at once that,

SURRENDER OF LORD CORNWALLIS

Clumsy hand-drawn forgery, intended to simulate a transfer print, applied to a genuine Wedgwood dish. Size, 8 x 10 inches. (See page 251.)

GEORGE WASHINGTON

Earthenware bust attributed to Enoch Wood. Height, 8 inches. Stafford shire, 1790. In the Willett Collection.

Modern forged copy of the Enoch Wood bust still being produced in quantities in Staffordshire. (See page 240.)

while the dish looked and felt like genuine Wedgwood, the decoration was certainly not Wedgwood. I asked him to send the dish to the factory at Etruria, and let me have a report on it. He was pleased to do so, and in a week or more I received a letter from the factory telling me all about it.

The verdict was that the ware is genuine Wedgwood of about 1840. The piece is the bottom part of a cushion shaped vegetable dish, belonging to a set made of plain cream ware, and undecorated except for a black line around the edge of each piece. The crude picture of the surrender of Cornwallis had been applied at a later period and the piece had been refired at a low heat. My informant concluded his report by saying: "We suffer in this respect today. So many amateurs like to dabble in ceramic painting. Having in most cases no technical knowledge, they get hold of our plain ware, almost always glazed ware, and decorate it,—in a few cases quite well, in most cases quite atrociously. Of course, in years to come, it will pass as Wedgwood, because it has our stamp upon it; but the fabric only is ours, the decoration is absolutely alien."

Trumbull's painting of the surrender of Cornwallis was completed in 1824. A steel engraving of it was made by Tanner in 1828, and Currier & Ives published a lithograph in colors of the subject in 1852. Either the engraving or the lithograph could have been used by the clumsy "amateur" who attempted to add a fictitious value to the plain cream-ware Wedgwood vegetable dish. The other "historical" pieces in that dealer's shop were, of course, of the same ilk.

When I got back to New York, a few months later, I visited the antique section of the department store whose astute buyer had purchased the six plates decorated with ships—for which he had paid about $4.87 per plate. I saw two of them—two of those I had seen in London—on display. The other four had been sold. I asked particularly about these, to make certain. The remaining two were priced at $150 apiece!

The faking and counterfeiting of pottery and furniture that is being done in England and other European countries today is principally for the American market. But in spite of all the faking, there is still much of the genuine to be found, and there are many honest dealers in whom one may place implicit trust. Indeed, the one the average collector has most to fear is himself. The desire to possess frequently blinds him to the danger signals he might otherwise perceive. Many of us, knowing full well that counterfeits are being offered at every hand, feel that we, at least, are not to be deceived. This is not exactly pedantry in most cases; it is an unfortunately natural faith in human nature which leads us to place too much trust in the soft persuasiveness of unscrupulous salesmen.

The only way to avoid too many mistakes is to study your subject thoroughly, to get to know your periods; to familiarize yourself with the characteristics of the objects you really want, to visit collections at every opportunity, to be patient and cautious, yet not always suspicious. Every one makes mistakes occasionally. No one can learn without making mistakes. But, after all, are not the recollections of some of the mistakes we have made among the pleasantest and most profitable of the memories of our collecting adventures?

POSTSCRIPT

IT is customary, in books of this nature, for the author to prefix a brief note, in the neighborhood of the title page, acknowledging his indebtedness to editors, publishers and others for permitting the reprinting of certain material contained in the book, or for assistance and advice in its preparation. Such notes are usually brief, and of no particular interest to the reader. They are a sop to conventionality,— a mere voluntary compliance with certain canons of courtesy, just as the printing of the copyright notice is a necessary compliance with the requirement of the law. And so, the author, having made his perfunctory bow, proceeds with his narrative,—and most of his readers have not even noticed the bow.

An old story comes to mind of the professor who asked a pupil for a definition of "preface." The young man replied that it was that part of a book which nobody read. Such is the attitude of youth. As we grow older, we come to realize that the preface is quite likely to be the *bonne bouche* of the entire volume. Here, indeed, is the intimate, the personal, rather than the formal word of the author. Here he may frequently whisper something that he might hesitate to pronounce in his more ponderous pages.

After all, it is of no particular value to the reader

to know, at the outset, that certain chapters of a book have previously appeared in print. Doubtless this actually annoys some people. Neither is the public interest particularly aroused by gratitude expressed to amiable individuals who may have been of real assistance to the author. Readers in general are not particularly interested in hearing grace before the meal,—they want to get right to the meat.

For these reasons, I have refrained from making formal acknowledgments alongside the copyright notice. It seems to me that the postscript is the more proper form. I can now, and here, admit that certain chapters in this book were originally published in *House and Garden* and *Country Life,* whose editors have been kind enough not to object to their inclusion in this volume. They have even gone further, and have generously allowed me to use photographs which were made for their own purpose. This is quite characteristic of editors, for I have never known one yet who quarreled with an author because he wanted to make further use of material which they themselves had considered of sufficient interest to publish. Such a proceeding is, in a sense, a confirmation of their own good judgment,—even if this judgment is only confirmed by one who might not be considered as wholly unbiased.

After all, the world is full of amiable and helpful people. If this were not so, few of us would ever learn much. Fortunately the gods have so willed it that those who have acquired knowledge, of whatever kind it may be, delight in passing it on to such others as may display a sincere desire to learn.

I was particularly impressed with this human characteristic in my contacts and association with antique dealers in England. A great many of these were extremely well informed. At first I tried to conceal my own ignorance by not asking too many questions, but I soon discovered that they were all cordially eager to give time and exert effort to instruct me in the mysteries of their own predominant interest. To these gentlemen, some whose names I now forget and many whose names I never even knew, I wish to express my sincere and thankful appreciation.

In a little junk-shop in Putney, where I was wandering one Saturday afternoon, I found a stoneware flask which was obviously a portrait, but I stupidly was unable to identify the character. Stupid is none too strong a word, for the flask portrayed Sir Herbert Asquith. The dealer was a Ceylonese and was not interested in portraiture. I took good care not to arouse his interest, as this might likewise have raised his price. I bought the piece for a couple of shillings, noting the impressed mark of "Doulton, Lambeth" on its base.

Through inquiries concerning this flask, I became acquainted with the Art Director of the Royal Doulton Works, who became a friend and adviser in the months that followed. By his aid I obtained many excellent specimens of salt-glazed stoneware, among them some of my most treasured specimens.

My brief visit to Staffordshire was made delightful by the hospitality and interest of the Curator of the Museum at Hanley, who spared no effort in conducting me throughout the Five Towns, affording me access to the minor potteries as well as to the several treasure houses of the earlier glories of Staffordshire, notably the little Wedgwood Museum at Etruria, whose amiable Curator opened up many little cabinets, the dusty little doors of which indicated that such privilege was not accorded to all comers.

To the Keeper of the Public Library, Museum and Fine Art Galleries, at Brighton, I am gratefully indebted for much information concerning the Willett Collection, as well as for the opportunity to obtain and to use in this volume photographs of specimens from that unique aggregation of British folk pottery.

I am similarly indebted to the Assistant Keeper of the Victoria and Albert Museum at South Kensington, and to the amiable officials of the Metropolitan Museum in New York, for much valuable guidance and assistance, as well as for permission to reproduce herein certain photographs of specimens in these collections.

Perhaps the greatest debt I have to acknowledge is that to my friend and fellow-collector in London whose home I have too often used as a sort of storage warehouse or receiving vault for pieces picked up here and there and dispatched to safekeeping in his care until such time as I could gather them unto mine own shelves.

It is apparent, therefore, that collecting has other charms than the mere acquisition of trophies. The thrill of the hunt and the joy of capture are surrounded on all sides and assisted at all times by a universal human kindness which almost puts the breath of life into our inanimate gatherings, and certainly renders unforgettable the incidents and associations of the joyful chase.

BIBLIOGRAPHY

A. B. C. of Collecting Old English Pottery. J. F. Blacker. London, Stanley Paul & Co.

The A. B. C. of English Salt Glaze Stoneware. J. F. Blacker. London, Stanley Paul & Co., 1922.

The Blue China Book. Ada Walker Camehl. New York, E. P. Dutton, 1916.

British Pottery Marks. G. Woolliscroft Rhead. London, Scott, Greenwood & Son, 1910.

Catalogue of American Potteries and Porcelains in the Pennsylvania Museum. Prepared by Edwin Atlee Barber. Philadelphia, 1893.

Catalogue of a Collection of English Pottery Figures in the Royal Museum and Art Galleries, Peel Park, Manchester. Manchester, Geo. Falkner & Sons, 1906.

Catalogue of a Collection of Pottery and Porcelain Illustrating Popular British History. (The Willett Collection) London, H. M. Stationery Office, 1899.

Catalogue of the Herbert Allen Collection of English Porcelain in the Victoria and Albert Museum. Bernard Rackham. London, 1923.

Catalogue of the Schreiber Collection of English Porcelain, Earthenware and Enamels in the Victoria and Albert Museum. Vol. I: Porcelain. Bernard Rackham. London, 1915.

Catalogue of the Schreiber Collection in the Victoria and Albert Museum. Vol. II: Earthenware. Bernard Rackham. London, 1930.

Catalogue of an Exhibition of Fakes and Reproductions Shown at the Pennsylvania Museum. Philadelphia, 1916.

Chats on English Earthenware. Arthur Hayden. London, T. Fisher Unwin, 1909.

The China Collector. H. William Lewer. London, Herbert Jenkins.

Collecting Old Lustre Ware. W. Bosanko. London, William Heinemann, 1916.

261

PORTRAITS IN POTTERY

The Earthenware Collector. G. Woolliscroft Rhead. London, Herbert Jenkins, 1920.

A Guide to the English Pottery and Porcelain in the British Museum. London, 1923.

Handbook of Marks and Monograms on Pottery and Porcelain. William Chaffers. London, Reeves & Turner, 1903.

History and Description of English Earthenware and Stoneware to the Beginning of the Nineteenth Century. W. Burton. London, 1904.

How to Identify Old China. Mrs. Willoughby Hodgson. London, George Bell & Sons, 1904.

Josiah Wedgwood: Master Potter. Sir A. H. Church. London, 1894.

Josiah Wedgwood and His Pottery. W. Burton. London, 1922.

List of Books and Pamphlets on Pottery and Porcelain Contained in the Lending and Reference Libraries of Stoke-on-Trent. Stoke, 1926.

Nineteenth Century English Ceramic Art. J. F. Blacker. London, Stanley Paul & Co.

Notes on the Willett Collection of Pottery in the Brighton Museum. H. Housman. Brighton, 1893.

A Picture Book of English Porcelain Figures. Victoria and Albert Museum. London, 1925.

Pink Lustre Pottery. Atwood Thorne. London, B. T. Batsford, Ltd., 1926.

Pottery and Porcelain of the United States. Edwin Atlee Barber. 1901.

Salt Glazed Stoneware. Edwin Atlee Barber. Philadelphia, 1906.

A Short History of Staffordshire Pottery. Stoke on Trent, 1926.

Staffordshire Pots and Potters. G. W. & F. A. Rhead. London, Hutchinson & Co., 1906.

The Potters and Potteries of Bennington. John Spargo. Boston, Houghton, Mifflin Co., 1926.

Staffordshire Pottery Figures. Herbert Read. London, Duckworth, 1929.

Transfer Printing on Enamels, Porcelain and Pottery. William Turner. London, Chapman & Hall, 1907.

The Wood Family of Burslem. F. Falkner. London, 1912.

Index

INDEX

INDEX

INDEX

INDEX

INDEX

—of the Belgians: 111
—of Sardinia: 216
—of Saxony: 64
—William III: 110
—William IV: 63, 69, 70, 73, 87, 88, 97, 111, 117, 130, 237, 240, 242
King St., London: 153, 165
King's Arms (inn, Godalming): 131, 134
—Road, London: 28, 31, 156
Kitchener, Lord: 54
Knightsbridge, London: 156
Knole: 150
Kosciuszko: 116

L

laces: 209
Lafayette: 5, 63, 68, 116, 247
Lakin & Poole: 115
Lamb, Charles: 117
Lambeth: 28, 31, 32, 48, 50, 51, 53, 57, 61, 73, 85, 87, 130, 168, 258
Lambeth-Delft: 109
Lane Delph: 234
late-Victorian period: 166, 237, 242
Latin Quarter, Paris: 194
Leda: 58
Leeds: 57, 68, 238, 239, 242, 250, 251
Lenox, Trenton, N. J.: 53
lettering, styles of: 74, 85, 243
Lincoln, Abraham: 84, 85, 238, 244
Lincoln's Inn Fields: 154
lion-tamer: 119
Little Eva: 82
Liverpool: 57, 61, 68, 107, 116, 238, 242
—Museum: 65, 68, 120
Lloyd George, David: 54, 55, 88
Locke, John: 117
London: 24, 25, 28, 57, 64, 123, 124, 148, 152-164, 165-185
—Museum: 33
Longacre, London: 154
long-beards: 44
Longfellow, H. W.: 85, 101, 117
Longton Hall: 78
Louvre Museum: 99, 190
Lowell, J. R.: 101
Lowestoft: 233
lustre cups: 212
—jugs: 211, 225, 226
—, silver: 227

M

Macbeth: 135

Madonnas: 60, 188, 189
Maidenhead: 150
Manchester: 121
man-jugs: 45
maps: 191
Marat: 115
Marlborough, Duke of: 114
—House: 165
Marché aux Puces: 197-200
Maty, Dr.: 162
McKinley, William: 53
medallions: 65
Meissen: 59, 99
Mercury: 58
Mersey Canal: 64
Metcalfe, Percy: 55
Metropolitan Museum of Art, N. Y.: 16, 39, 47, 92, 95, 250, 259
Mexico: 11, 45
Midhurst: 146
mid-Victorian period: 71, 85, 90, 120, 218, 221, 237, 241, 242, 244
Milton: 62, 65, 117, 137, 161, 162, 243
Ming dynasty: 58
mistakes: 184, 254, 255
Mitre (inn, Hampton Court): 150
Mohammed: 201
Montenegro: 102
Montmartre: 197, 210
Moore, Sir John: 115
Morand, Paul: 186, 190
Morgan, Mr. J. P.: 16
Mory's chophouse: 11
Motley, J. L.: 142
mourning pieces: 111
"Mrs. Caudle's Curtain Lectures": 89
mugs: 69, 73, 114, 116, 233
Munroe, Sir Hector: 118
MUSEUMS: American Museum of Natural History, New York: 45, 203; British Museum, London, 16, 62, 109, 161, 162, 170; Cluny, Musée de, Paris, 187; Hanley Public Museum and Art Gallery, 90, 259; Louvre, Paris, 99, 190; London Museum, 33; Liverpool Museum, 65, 68, 120; Metropolitan Museum of Art, New York, 16, 39, 47, 92, 95, 250, 259; Museum of Practical Geology, London, 92, 93, 94; Public Library, Museums and Fine Art Galleries, Brighton, 108, 259; Royal Museum and Art Gallery, Manchester, 121; Royal Porcelain Works Museum, Worcester, 68;

INDEX

INDEX

270

INDEX

S

Saints: 60
St. Albans: 126, 127, 128, 129, 141
St. George and the Dragon: 62, 141
St. Germain Fair: 193
St. Germain des Près: 193
St. James' St., London: 153, 154
St. Malo: 209, 211
St. Paul's Cathedral: 147
St. Vincent, battle of: 235
Salisbury: 125, 126, 141, 142, 143, 145
Salt, Ralph: 71
Saxon factories: 59, 60, 99
Saxony, King of: 64
Scandinavia: 122
Schreiber Collection: 17
—Lady Constance: 17
Scotland: 96
Scott, Dr.: 74, 75, 76
Scott, Sir Walter: 96, 117
Scottish National Portrait Gallery: 163
Second Empire: 238
Seneca: 65
Sergeant, John: 164
Sevenoaks: 150
Seven Years' war: 93
Sèvres: 59, 60, 99
Shaftesbury Ave., London: 155
Shakespeare: 117, 162, 179
Shelton: 61
Shepherd's Bush: 158, 171, 172, 173, 176, 180, 184
—Market, London: 153
ship models: 148, 209, 210
silver: 153
Skindle's (inn, Maidenhead): 150
Sloane Square, London: 156
Slough: 140
Smith, Governor Alfred E.: 54, 55
—Sir Sidney: 113
Snuff-Taker: 46
Soane & Smith: 54
South Kensington: 17, 73
Southey, Robert: 76
Southsea: 148, 149
Spain: 188, 189
Spargo, John: 48
Spode: 49, 78
Sports and Sporting: 118, 222
Spread Eagle (inn, Midhurst): 146, 147
Staffordshire: 11, 37, 39, 41, 46, 47, 48, 49, 50, 54, 57, 61, 66, 67, 71, 73, 77, 78, 79, 80, 81, 82, 84, 85, 87, 90, 91, 98, 102, 107, 110, 111, 115, 119, 120, 135, 171, 211, 214, 215, 216, 218, 222, 223, 226, 234, 236, 238, 239, 245, 259
Staffordshire-Delft: 107, 109
Staple Inn: 154
Starkey, J. S. W.: 52
statuettes: 71, 79, 81
Sterne, Lawrence: 42
Stevenson & Williams: 68
Stoke-on-Trent: 49, 117, 120, 227
Stoke Poges: 136, 138
Stonehenge: 145
stoneware, English: 36, 87, 130
—Flemish: 44
—French: 213
—German: 44
Stowe, Mrs. Harriet Beecher: 82, 84, 117
Sultan Abdul Medjid: 80
Sunderland: 57, 68, 212, 224, 226, 228
—jugs: 18, 68, 223, 224

T

Tanagra figurines: 58
Tanner: 253
tapestries: 154
teacups: 233
—Japanese ceremonial: 231
teapots: 77, 112, 234
Temple, the: 165
Tennyson, Alfred: 86, 101
terminology: 33
terre de Jersey: 211, 212, 213, 227
Thames, the: 140
Theobald's Road, London: 154
Thompson, Joseph: 90
Thun: 8, 11, 218
tobacco jars: 180
Toby-jugs: 39, 42, 51, 153
Toft, James, Thomas & Ralph: 61
toothpicks: 201-202
toy soldiers: 203, 204, 205
Trafalgar, battle of: 75, 114, 148, 235
transfer printing: 65, 66, 85, 251
Tree, Sir Herbert: 164
"Tristram Shandy": 42
"Tristram Shandy" jug: 224
Trollope, Capt.: 235
Trouville: 212
Trumbull Gallery: 251
—John: 251, 253
Tunbridge Wells: 150
Turkey: 79, 80, 113, 216
Turner: 78
"Twelfth Night": 179

271

INDEX

O.S